Endorsements for

The Journey After the Journeys

Teresa's life is a true testament to the adage: "Do what you *love*, and *love* what you do." *The Journey After the Journeys* is riveting and will inspire you to say *yes* to fulfilling the Great Commission. It will challenge you to step out of your comfort zone, while you walk through a journey of discovery to find your ultimate Sole Purpose. Be prepared to be transformed.

Emmanuel "Manny" Ohonme
Co-Founder, President, CEO
Samaritan's Feet International
North Carolina

If anyone can take you on a journey to get to know the lost, unseen, and hopeless, it's Teresa. Over the years, she has told me about her many travels in the most primitive of areas in our world. I've often wondered why she does it. Why go?

Then, Teresa, through Samaritan's feet, offered to bring shoes to one of our low-income school districts here in Florida. She invited me to serve on her team. While I was sitting on the floor replacing kids' smelly, too tight, worn out and passed down shoes with new shoes, I got it! Their eyes lit up, and some of them danced across the floor. What grabbed my heart the most wasn't the impact it made on the kids. It was seeing Teresa sitting on the floor as well. What a huge heart she has to be willing to sacrifice so much time away from her own family to fly anywhere; sleep in tents, the ground or whatever was offered; and live with or without indoor plumbing in order to provide shoes that not only fit, but make life much easier for so many.

I urge you to read her many journeys because as you do you will be inspired, brought to tears, encouraged, and challenged to make a difference in your part of the world like you never have before.

Pastor Kim Anderson
Discipleship Director
Bayside Community Church
Florida

As I began to read *The Journey After the Journeys,* I immediately felt engaged and compelled. The book drew me in to continue reading, and it challenged me about my own actions in communicating the love of God to a hurting world. This is a book that needed to be written. I am so thankful Teresa Hucko has taken on this work to challenge us.

I've often looked at crisis situations in the world and asked myself, "How can I make a difference?" I see in *The Journey After the Journeys* that maybe I've been asking the wrong question. Instead of focusing on the problem, I should focus more on the individuals that I can reach, those I can help.

Teresa does this as she shares from her life her struggles with massive world problems that she cannot fix. She has found herself in the midst of the people experiencing crisis firsthand and found she was able to make a difference in individual lives. Her life has impacted so many. As you read *The Journey After the Journeys* you'll be challenged to enter into your own journey in a life of significance.

Underground Church Pastor
who has worked abroad with Teresa Hucko

The Journey **After** the Journeys

Your bags are unpacked—but your journey is not over!

Teresa Hucko

HIGHWAY 51
PUBLISHING

Published by Highway 51 Publishing, LLC
Mint Hill, North Carolina
HWY51.com

ISBN: 0-9960570-8-0
ISBN-13: 978-0-9960570-8-0

Cover design: Ruth Russell
Editing: Kristen Driscoll, Highway 51 Publishing

This is My Journey After the Journeys

As I resist my knowledge of the unjust, the evil, the hopeless.
As I process my fear, my grief, my sadness.
As I embrace kindness, goodness, faithfulness.

—Teresa Hucko

Thank you, my Heavenly Father.
Thank you for being faithful to me over the years.
Thank you for my many beautiful journeys.

To my best friend, my husband, Greg
I am grateful for our journey,
and I want to thank you for supporting me in my journeys.

For my children AJ and Meg, Alysse and Harry
For my grandchildren Lily, Isabel, Clark, and Violet
(and hopefully others to come!)
You have given me immeasurable JOY in my journey.

Contents

Foreword

"How beautiful are the feet of those that bring good news!"
—Romans 10:15, NIV

Let me begin by acknowledging the phenomenal, raw, real, and impactful words and work of this project from the heart of my dear friend, Teresa Hucko. The message in *The Journey After the Journeys* leaps off the pages and into your soul.

The definition of the word *journey* is "to travel from one place to another." It usually means traveling a long distance, often in dangerous and difficult circumstances. *Journey* can also include the passage from youth to maturity, or a trip through time. Both definitions invoke a process of movement, growth, and evolving from our daily existence into a place of intentional living. It means to go beyond, to venture out, to explore, to learn.

We each must be brave enough to take the journey from the place of comfort to the unfamiliar and unknown—where our fear meets up with our faith. What we say with our mouth, we must believe with our hearts to achieve. The stories in this book share a common thread of determination and hope, woven through the individuals Teresa has met on her journey.

Teresa, and you and I, all have a common thread, too—a thread of opportunity. Each of us can share our story and the stories of others that need to be heard and felt, so that others can empathize with a world in need of love and understanding—one we can value, and see beyond the circumstances and surroundings and into the heart of others.

Teresa does all of that through her stories: From camping in Kenya, to the refugee camps in Greece, to the side roads of Morocco, to the untouchables in India, each chapter captures your emotions, tests your faith walk, and challenges your intellect. These are real people, children of the one true King. From marginalized girls and women, to young boys and girls in crowded work camps, to displaced and fractured families seeking a better life, we come to understand that we must not look upon them—or those like them—with a savior mentality. We have to approach from a place of honest and authentic relationship, while truly understanding that poverty is not just a socio-economic problem, but also one of the spirit.

Mother Teresa says it best: "We think sometimes that poverty is only being hungry, naked, and homeless. The poverty of being unwanted, unloved, and uncared for is the greatest poverty. ... Let us touch the dying, the poor, the lonely, and the unwanted according to the graces we have received and let us not be ashamed or slow to do the humble work."

In our own journeys, we each have potential to serve, engage, invest, and inspire. For Teresa, it was serving as a children's pastor for many years. That is where our paths crossed, and we began to form a friendship that years later would allow us to serve together through Samaritan's Feet International. The ministry offers the simple impact of washing people's feet and gifting them shoes, but it leaves a lasting imprint far beyond the life of the shoes. It's an exchange of mutual transformation.

From one woman to another, we have a responsibility to pave the path we hope others will follow, making the world a better place for the next generation. This book is a step toward that goal. As Mother Teresa said, "I alone cannot change the world, but I can cast a stone across the waters to create many ripples."

Tracie Ohonme
Co-Founder and Executive Vice President
Samaritan's Feet International

If I Could Hit a Button …

*"… I am he, I am he who will sustain you. I have made you and I
will carry you; I will sustain you and I will rescue you."*
—*Isaiah 46:4, NIV*

If I could hit a button and not know all that I know
now—I'm afraid I would be tempted to do so. It's easier to
live in a small, contained world, to be unaware of the
hardships of many—both in my backyard and around the
globe.

But there is no such button.

And, for some reason, God has trusted me with this
information, this burden. I have traveled extensively, and in
my earlier travels I encountered poverty. But as long as there
was food, family, and hope, I always saw joy. However, my
more recent travels exposed me to situations that were more
difficult, even hopeless. I saw poverty of the soul.

I met refugees detained in camps who were angry and
sad. Hopeless. They could not go home, and it was very
difficult to move forward. There was no music. No singing.
No school. I was not allowed to take photos.

I couldn't fix it.

At one point, I found myself holding a starving baby
while her sibling lay dying in a makeshift tent. I had very little
to give to the mother. It wasn't a scheduled stop. I was
unprepared for a complicated, overwhelming situation.

I couldn't fix it.

Another time, I was serving hot food to children who had

no plates. They simply held open their tender hands for the hot rice mixture, their only food for the day. I scanned the ground for anything—paper, leaves, I didn't care how dirty it was—I just wanted something to protect their hands from the hot food.

I couldn't fix it.

At a boarding school, I instinctively knew something was wrong. The children seemed traumatized, quiet. Then, I learned their story.

I couldn't fix it.

These circumstances and others like them changed me. Often, if I'm honest, it leaves me heavyhearted. I think, "If only I could hit a button and not know all I have been exposed to … would I?" It would tempt me.

I work hard, but after the work is done, I return home to my beautiful family, lovely home, sweet friends, and co-workers. I eat out—a lot. I shop at nice malls, get my nails done, and color my hair. I indulge my grandchildren and rest at my oceanfront condo.

But in the quiet, I grieve. I pray. And I ask why? Why, God, have you allowed me to see this? What is required of me? What can I do? There is so much that I cannot fix. It paralyzes me.

I look to God's word, as it must have an answer. It does, and in this book I'll share with you His answers to me.

This is my journey after the journeys, as I learn to embrace my knowledge of the unfair and strive to make some small difference—as I choose not to hit that button.

Part One

Your bags are unpacked—
but your journey is not over.

Chapter 1

Why Are You Here?

Be kind to one another, tenderhearted, forgiving one another,
as God in Christ forgave you.
—Ephesians 4:32

This was my first visit to Morocco. I always enjoyed the food, the sights, and especially the hospitality of those I met across Africa. This was true of Morocco, as well. During our journey across the country, we stopped at the city of Chefchaouen. This storybook town's narrow streets were peppered with ancient buildings painted a dramatic "Carolina Blue." The arched doorways, *mashrabiya* windows, ornate city gates, and quaint shops added to the charm. The streets were lined with bags of brightly colored spices, and a pleasant aroma wafted from sidewalk vendors selling sweets. Breathtaking. Sipping mint tea on a rooftop restaurant, I could imagine Aladdin on a magic carpet, swooping through this very ancient Arabian village. In fact, it felt like one of the towns from which Disney would model such a scene.

Most of my trips came about through the connections of Samaritan's Feet. This trip was the exception. K-LOVE Radio had run a feature on Samaritan's Feet, when I was serving as the organization's International Director.

The ministry is centered on washing the feet of people in need, offering them prayer, and fitting them with new shoes. In his book *Sole Purpose*, Manny Ohonme tells the beautiful story of how he and his wife, Tracie, founded Samaritan's Feet. Manny grew up in Nigeria, and he received his first pair of shoes at age nine at a basketball camp run by a short-term mission team. The shoes were the most valuable possession that he had ever owned. Years later, Manny came to the United States on a basketball scholarship. He never forgot that feeling of getting his first pair of shoes and, eventually, he and his wife felt a call into full-time ministry. Manny used the memory of his experience to turn the gift of shoes into a tool to spread hope. At this writing, Samaritan's Feet is a little more than 15 years old. They have sent shoes to 108 countries, served in more than 385 U.S. cities, and distributed almost seven million pairs of shoes!

Pastor Bob, an American missionary serving in Morocco, was visiting family in Atlanta. He heard Manny's story and the mission of Samaritan's Feet on K-Love Radio. He emailed me with the story of how immigrants from all over Africa had entered Morocco. They were living in the woods and had very few provisions. They had walked hundreds of miles, and, of course, after that they needed shoes.

Unfortunately, I received many such emails. Bob's email was well written but not overwhelmingly compelling. I had a standard reply to such messages that went something like this: "The needs are many, and the resources are limited. If the opportunity comes for us to expand, I will keep your information on file and be in touch … ." However, every time I went to write that reply and file the contact in my "abyss folder," the Holy Spirit stopped me. I simply could not process and file his email.

After a couple of weeks, I mentioned this opportunity to Manny. He encouraged me to vet the contact. I did, and Pastor Bob was quick to fill out our extensive paperwork and provide me with several references. Amazingly, the one person I knew from his home state actually *knew* his reference. Many emails and many months later, I had assembled the first team of seven for an exploratory trip to Morocco.

I had no idea how deeply this trip would challenge me. It started preparing me for my future trips. This became a defining moment, a dividing line in time for my trips prior to Morocco and my trips after.

At this point, I already was a seasoned traveler. As an international director for a faith-based organization, I had organized and led more mission trips than I could count. The trips revealed many difficult circumstances and profound poverty. I had visited orphans, helped with feeding programs, engaged in training conferences, sponsored children, and handed out water-filtration systems. I danced and sang and played with children. We left offerings to support the ongoing work. I would return home tired but with a full heart and a joyful team. I had no reason to expect that this excursion would be any different.

The itinerary included a great deal of travel to various cities across Morocco. Our host had lived in Morocco for more than 15 years. He actually rode his Harley Davidson motorcycle from one end of the country to the other. He knew it well.

We started the week attending a church where we could worship freely. Pastor Bob's church is for expatriates living in the country. Many of his congregants are teachers at English-speaking schools; others are immigrants working various jobs in Morocco. I learned that a government official could show up at the doors to his church on any given Sunday and ask to see the passports of those entering. If the person has a foreign passport, they are permitted to enter. However, all citizens of Morocco are required to be Muslim, so it is illegal for them to attend the Christian church. But even in this circumstance, God has a plan. A simple passport check—or worse—will not keep His church from growing. God is drawing people to His church through a network of pastors and churches, and it's not in church buildings. God is changing lives and dispensing the hope of salvation.

We traveled to three cities and did a basic outreach event and supply distribution at a church in each one. Our recipients were mainly poor immigrants who attended the churches. We offered prayer to all who came. The events were beautiful but somewhat standard for someone like me who frequently oversees similar events. That was about to change, though.

One day in October 2013, we made our way to the northernmost tip of Morocco, near the border of Spain. During this long, winding drive, our missionary host explained that migrants and refugees from various parts of Africa were living in the woods there. They had traveled hundreds of miles, mainly from Sub-Saharan Africa to this spot. I was unaware of the flood of people fleeing West Africa. Some were fleeing war and gangs, while others were fleeing poverty. All of them were seeking a better life, if they could just reach Europe.

A narrow strip of water less than nine miles wide separates the continent of Africa from Europe. You can stand in Morocco, look over the Mediterranean Sea, and easily spot the Rock of Gibraltar in Spain. To many, Europe represents a chance at a new life. Some try to cross on overloaded boats. Many of the boats capsize, resulting in tragedy and death. They have come so far and just when it seems as if their journey is almost over, they meet with disaster.

Another lesser-known fact is that two Spanish cities lie on the northern shore of Morocco's Mediterranean coast. Ceuta, a tiny Spanish territory, lies just eighteen miles across the water from Gibraltar, and 250 miles farther down the Moroccan coast sits Melilla. Together, they form the European Union's only land border with Africa. Because of this proximity to Europe, many migrants travel to this area. They live in the woods and form makeshift camps as they make plans to enter Europe by land or by sea.

Our first stop? It literally was the side of the road. I like to call it the "Drive-By Distribution." It was much, much more than that, though. We simply pulled our van to the side of the road, spread a bright blue paint tarp on the ground, and pulled out a couple of folding chairs. Our missionary friend called out, and, little by little, young men emerged from the woods. We wiped each man's feet with baby wipes and fitted them with a new pair of shoes. We then offered prayer, which they each accepted. I use the word *men*, but they were young. Most were teens; some were younger. They were smiling ear to ear. Looking back, I know they desperately needed the new shoes, but they needed a kind touch even more. That day, they received both.

Toward the end of this distribution, the local military interrupted us. We had just finished serving about a hundred of the men. As the military vehicles quickly advanced on us, the men scattered and ran into the woods. Very quickly, about ten men armed with pistols and MP5 rifles surrounded us. I'll never forget one teammate who just sat on the tarp, not frozen with fear but likely just too tired to stand at that point. He simply looked at me with amusement on his face. If he'd had a thought bubble, I think it would have read: "Now what are you going to do, Teresa?"

My bubble would have been completely blank. I had no idea what we should do!

A small-statured man, whom I privately referred to as "Al Capone," was in charge of the soldiers. He insisted on collecting our passports. Our work completely confused him. He couldn't comprehend why someone would want to help "those people" in the woods. While it is illegal to give rides or cash to the immigrants, we were doing neither; after about 45 minutes and a lot of explaining from our host, our passports were returned.

When I share this experience, I am often asked, "Were you scared?" I can truly say that I was not. We were smiling. The team was completely peaceful. Being detained on the side of the road and having our passports confiscated by "Al Capone" and a squad from the local military base just became part of the day. The military leader finally released us. The soldiers left, and we continued to our next location.

I sometimes use the word *immigrant* or *migrant* and sometimes the word *refugee*. While I do not know if the people here were "official refugees," I do know most were trying to escape some very difficult situations. Many felt that if they did not flee from their homeland, they would certainly die. It's complicated. The next part of this story is compiled from what I was told and what I saw.

My most recent interaction showed me that many Moroccans were not happy with the immigrants. They simply wanted them to go away.

We entered a makeshift camp of more than a hundred people, this time including women and children. The missionary pointed to burn marks on the ground while he was talking to a camp leader. The leader explained what had happened a few days before we arrived.

Late one night, while everyone was sleeping, a group of men whom the leader suspected to be military officials had come into the woods and set their tents on fire. Chaos rained down on the immigrants as they ran out of their tents. Some said they were beaten with clubs while their attackers shouted, "Go back home!"

I now recognized on the ground burn mark after burn mark after burn mark. What few possessions these displaced people had … gone. Once the people started to appear, I saw their bruises and that they had nothing. I truly cannot put into words the heaviness in the camp at that moment, but I had a great team. We drew from a deep inner strength and set to work preparing with that same blue tarp. We planned to serve the women and children first. We sat on the bags the shoes came in and again used baby wipes and lotion on each person's feet before fitting them with new shoes. Most smiled and laughed as we served them. All welcomed prayer. Simple items like balloons brought the children a little fun and distraction from what had become a harsh life. This kindness was foreign to most of them. Their current world was not kind.

I was sitting next to a sweet team member, a soft-spoken pastor's wife from North Carolina. Then, in perfect English, the man she was serving asked, "Why are you here?"

She simply replied, "I'm here to tell you God loves you."

He repeated, "God loves me? "

"Yes," she softly replied, "God loves you." She was

completely sincere and pure in heart, that I know. However, this conversation haunted me. How could this man, in his current circumstances, understand that God loves him? How do we remind people that they are not forgotten, and that God does love them, and at the same time stay sensitive to their circumstances? How do we make sure our actions and the words we speak benefit those we are serving and do not just make us feel good about ourselves?

As we served this community of a hundred, we received word that the people of another camp were heading our way. We didn't have enough of the sizes needed. The current group didn't understand the concept of standing in line. The blue tarp was meant only for those we were serving at that moment, but many kept crowding around us. If you are even slightly claustrophobic, that does not feel good. *Next time,* I thought, *I'll bring my handy-dandy caution tape!* It does wonders, but in this situation it probably would not have helped, either.

Finally, the missionary decided that we needed to leave—**immediately**. He wanted us to be gone before others arrived, and rightly so, because we did not want the people to riot. We left huge bags of rice and oil—enough for the entire camp—and then we hurriedly pulled out. Others desperately wanting what we had made us sad, because we had more to give, but safety had to come first.

Much of my work has taken place in areas with great poverty, yet there was often much joy because the people still had hope. This situation felt different. These were desperate people who had very little. I don't think I had ever seen such desperation.

At first, I sat quietly, struggling within myself. I was fixated on the conversation that took place next to me, those words spoken by my sweet teammate. I thought:

I know, that I know, that I know that God does love them. But what if I were them? Would I believe that? Would I believe that God loved me, if I were broken, beaten, and cold—and had nothing? My tent burned, and my body bruised, and unable to protect my family? If that were my life, would I believe that God loves me? I'm now on my way to eat a full meal, sip on tea, and sleep in a clean hotel room. This is hard to rectify. I don't want to be a trite Christian, one who doesn't think about the hard questions ... .

I felt so conflicted. I was the team leader. I'd been to Bible school and had been in ministry for 25 years. I shared my struggle privately with my missionary friend. He answered:

"Teresa, these people had seen such little kindness. They were gathering around because they could not believe what they were seeing. Today, you washed feet and gave socks, shoes, and food. Even those who were not served *saw* what you did. When they ask, 'Who was kind to us?' they will remember the Christians who came and gave shoes."

Sometimes, problems are so big that there is no immediate cure. Their resolution is so far beyond my capabilities. But, I can be kind. That day, I had to let kindness be enough. This birthed in me the importance of simple acts of kindness.

I will always support ministries to orphans, training conferences, clean water, feeding programs, and microenterprise through sustainable, reputable organizations. Yet, I now see the importance of what I call "triage trips" to share kindness in impossible situations. This was preparing my heart.

Later that night, we went to a grocery store. We filled

hundreds of bags with basic groceries and hygiene products. It brought great joy on our return trip, as we slowly made our way down the narrow, curved roads, to see those we had served the previous day. I easily recognized their shoes.

We pulled over, and they ran up to the van where we passed the bags of food through the window. The day before, we had done a drive-by shoe distribution. Now we reversed our American drive-through! It was a simple thing we could do.

While I wish I had the knowledge and resources to make permanent changes and combat the systemic issues at the root of situations like this, I possess neither. The food would be gone in a few days. The shoes would wear out in time. Our help did not change their lives forever.

But, maybe it did. That day, they each knew that someone cared. The Christians who had prayed for them cared. They gave them shoes and food. They were kind. Maybe these distressed people would want to explore what it would be like to have a relationship with the God of the Christians.

"The Lord is near to the brokenhearted and saves the crushed in spirit."
—Psalm 34:18

Chefchaouen

Child in camp

Drive-by food giveaway

Chapter 2

Jail Bird

And everyone who has left houses or brothers or sisters or father or mother or children or lands, for my name's sake, will receive a hundredfold and will inherit eternal life.
—Matthew 19:29

When I think back to the many amazing people I have been privileged to meet in my life, this one lunch in Morocco will always stand out. Pastor Bob had asked if we wanted to meet and encourage an underground pastor.

"Why, *yes!*" I immediately answered. So, there we were on a busy street in Casablanca, seated and waiting at a Chinese restaurant. In walks a small, ordinary man. He caught Bob's eye. They smiled and hugged, and quickly he was seated. As our food was served, he began telling us how his church was growing and of their many needs.

Pastor Bob had been in Morocco for 15 years, and not once had he been able to visit "Pastor Sam's" church. And Pastor Sam could never be seen at Pastor Bob's church. Pastor Bob was an American living in the country. His church is for people like him, those who are from somewhere else. As I explained earlier, a government official can show up at the doors to his church on any given Sunday and ask to see the passports of those attending. Foreign passport holders are allowed to enter, but Moroccan passport holders cannot. Pastor Sam is a citizen of Morocco who is required to follow Islam. How I have taken my freedom to worship for granted!

Pastor Sam had given his life to Christ. As a former Muslim, it cost him. He lost his job, as well as his relationship with his parents and other family members. I asked if he was fearful that his parents would expose him. No, he explained, they love their grandchildren, and because they want to spend time with them, they keep his secret. Oh, the love of a grandparent!

When the pastor's children shared their faith at school once, they were severely threatened. While Pastor Sam does not live in fear, he does live with the knowledge that his choice to be a Christian has consequences. I think about that statement. Does my decision to follow Christ carry consequences? It should.

Pastor Sam works to equip the church and trains other Muslim believers. If caught, he would face incredible punishment. He desires to train pastors and leaders right in Morocco, rather than having them leave the country for training, as most of the time these future leaders do not return. It's a difficult task to perform in a Muslim nation, and he told us that his greatest need was for discipleship materials. Fortunately, Pastor Bob was able to gather many for him, and, to this day, Pastor Sam continues to equip and support the work of the underground church.

When we asked for prayer requests, the pastor asked us to pray that the words he shared would be effective. We gave funds to help, and I am sure many on the team are still praying for the effectiveness of this great man of faith, as well as supporting his efforts with resources today. I am grateful and inspired to have met such a strong hero of the faith.

I visited him again the following year, this time in his home. I sipped the hot mint tea and nibbled on the cookies his children sweetly served us. He was excited to share his church's progress: Hundreds have come to Christ, and at this writing there are now 25 underground pastors in their network! And it is growing every day. He expects to go to jail at least once a year, and he had just recently been released. The authorities know who he is, even if they don't comprehend the extent of his ministry. Yet, none of that deters his efforts. Instead, the kindness of the Christians is planting seeds. Kindness has an eternal value long after the items wear out and the food is gone. Kindness is simple. It is valuable. It is now my mantra: *Just be kind!*

About midnight Paul and Silas were praying and singing hymns to God, and the prisoners were listening to them.
—Acts 16:25

Chapter 3

They Look Like Us!

When a stranger sojourns with you in your land,
you shall not do him wrong.
—Leviticus 19:33

I went to speak to a class of students about my experiences. I've spoken in many places but, honestly, I was regretting saying yes this time. This wasn't a chapel or a special assembly. It was a school club called "Jr. Disciples," composed of a classroom of fifth grade students who met during their lunchtime. The club is modeled on the quote attributed to Saint Teresa of Avila that says that we are God's hands and feet on earth. It seemed that day, though, that many of the children were more interested in trading their snacks than listening to me share the needs of children from Africa. I had such a full schedule, and I questioned my decision, feeling pressure to complete more important tasks. It seemed like a complete waste of my time. I was very wrong.

The room mom was excited that I was coming. She had been persistent about getting a date that I could come to speak. She had met Manny at a Chinese New Year's Eve party and received one of his business cards. Then the communication began! She was intrigued by the ministry and told me she wanted to expose the children to our organization.

This is my first memory of Gina: a feisty, beautiful, Greek woman with a heart that beats for those less fortunate. Nothing holds Gina down, not even multiple sclerosis, a disease that she hides well, even though it makes walking difficult. In short, I couldn't say no to her. She helped the children collect items for my future trips, and her enthusiasm was genuine.

I immediately liked Gina and was glad I met her. We kept in touch. She brought in supplies to donate. Her family came to volunteer at our office. Then, a few months later, she showed up at my office, desperate. It was March 2015.

"Teresa, I must tell you what is happening on the Greek Island of Lésvos," Gina pleaded. "They are coming by the hundreds." Her friend from college lived on Lésvos and ran her family's beautiful coastal hotel, The Aphrodite Hotel, named for the Greek goddess, who was also her namesake. It doesn't get any more Greek than that. Gina had spoken to her friend on the phone: Aphrodite was overwhelmed by numbers of Syrian refugees landing on her beach.

In 2015, the number of migrants arriving in Greece reached record levels. According to the UNHCR, boats carried 660,000 people to the shores of Greece. At one point, approximately 4,500 people arrived per day. Most were coming from areas of deadly conflict such as Syria, Afghanistan, and Iraq. The island of Lésvos received the most arrivals, nearly 432,000. This influx placed a great strain on the 86,000 residents of this quiet tourist island. Reception and processing centers quickly overflowed capacity, as did shelter and sanitation capabilities. Beach rescue stories filled the news—some tales of success, others of tragic endings.

Life vests lined the beaches like washed up driftwood or sea shells. Someone had to clean it up daily, so the residents could somehow salvage their tourist season.

"Gina, they look like us!" Aphrodite said. "They have children and babies and grandmothers with them. They have nothing, and they are wet and cold." She continued, "Today, a raft with only children arrived on my beach!" Aphrodite took clothing from her own children's dressers and helped the refugee children to change. One young man exited the raft, and then gave Aphrodite his cell phone.

"Can you please call my father and tell him where I am?" he asked in broken English. Aphrodite wept as she tried to communicate this son's location to his family. Some of the Syrians did not understand that they had landed on an island.

When Gina hung up the phone, she cried on and off all day. She imagined the rafts landing on the same beach where she had vacationed many times. She was unsure of *what* she could do but knew she wanted to do *something*. That night, she awoke at 2:30 a.m. to a dream, a voice. The voice was loud, almost screaming—nearly audible she thought. The voice stated two simple things: "You know what to do!" and "You know how to do it!"

In her heart, Gina knew that it was Lord speaking to her. She was convinced that she needed to help both the Greeks living on Lésvos—many were losing everything to the refugee crisis—as well as the refugees themselves.

> *In the last days, God says, I will pour out my Spirit on all people.*
> *Your sons and daughters will prophesy, your young men will see visions,*
> *your old men will dream dreams.*
> —Acts 2:17, NIV

Gina shared her story with me. In 1999, she met her husband, Paul. She was excited to be engaged to be married; however, her health suffered from the complications of MS. About every eight weeks, she found herself in the hospital. Doctors put her on steroids and did a chemotherapy treatment to re-boot her immune system. Gina was not really a churchgoer then, but she found herself at church on the day of the "Blessing of the Sick."

She stood up and sincerely prayed, "God, please make me feel better, and I will serve you." It was a private prayer but an intentional one. Gina's health had improved. Now, she was married and had two children. She was leading a very active life, and when she had the dream, she immediately remembered her prayer years earlier.

Gina decided she must go to help. She had every excuse not to go: Her children were in elementary school and had busy schedules; a trip would cost money; and she had MS! But the dream, the voice, and her prayer compelled her to go.

This process built Gina's faith. Paul was supportive, so she emailed the organization I worked for to ask for supplies. Our founders quickly agreed, and she left with five huge duffle bags holding 200 pairs of shoes, 1,500 pairs of socks, and additional supplies. It was more luggage than any airline would allow one person to bring, but did I mention that she was feisty? She convinced the powers-that-be of the importance of every bag, and off to Greece she went.

When Gina returned to my office after her trip, she was no longer asking for a few bags of supplies. "We must go," she said. "You must put together a group of people, and we need to bring them to help. It's not stopping."

My calendar was set for the year. It takes months to arrange vetting, to gather contacts, to gather recruits. The list goes on and on. Gina wanted to go in a few short months. She didn't understand the magnitude of the request and the responsibility of taking a group. Going as an individual is one thing. Being responsible for a group of people in an unpredictable environment is very different, especially for a location I had never been to and where I had no experience. But in my heart, I knew: I was going to Greece.

What I imagined would be a small team of less than ten on an exploratory trip, turned into a team of 27. This team is a sampling of what I think heaven will be like. We had Greek Orthodox, Catholic, Baptist, Pentecostal, and non-denominational teammates. Mothers and daughters came, and sons, married couples, and singles, as well as my own adult daughter. We all were serving side by side.

The trip was difficult. It was challenging to see, to smell, to hear what was happening. The living conditions of the refugees were beyond crowded. There was no relief from the heat. Hopelessness hung in the air as the realization slowly dawned on the refugees that truly finding a new home and a new life was a complicated, slow process. Families were separated. Refugees carried tales of lives lost during the journey with no time to stop and grieve before pushing on. Former college students, professionals, and business owners now lived in tents. They wanted to work, to continue education, but their lives had stopped—and so had their will to live.

Our team was strong; we laughed at times until we cried. We worked hard, we prayed, we distributed shoes and food, we cleaned beaches, and we even danced! We came back changed. My memories and thoughts may not represent everyone else's. We each had our own experiences. My experience was that I now had the opportunity to see if the

power of kindness—that had so gripped my spirit in
Morocco—would transfer to this growing crisis in Greece.

The Good Samaritan

> *Jesus replied, "A man was going down from
> Jerusalem to Jericho, and he fell among robbers,
> who stripped him and beat him and departed,
> leaving him half dead. Now by chance a priest
> was going down that road, and when he saw him
> he passed by on the other side. So likewise a
> Levite, when he came to the place and saw him,
> passed by on the other side.*
>
> *But a Samaritan, as he journeyed, came to
> where he was, and when he saw him, he had
> compassion. He went to him and bound up his
> wounds, pouring on oil and wine. Then he set him
> on his own animal and brought him to an inn
> and took care of him.*
>
> *And the next day he took out two denarii and
> gave them to the innkeeper, saying, 'Take care of
> him, and whatever more you spend, I will repay
> you when I come back.' Which of these three, do
> you think, proved to be a neighbor to the man
> who fell among the robbers?" He said, "The one
> who showed him mercy." And Jesus said to him,
> "You go, and do likewise."* —Luke 10:30-37

Gina and Teresa

Gina and Aphrodite

Chapter 4

Numbers Talk!

And the Lord answered me "Write the vision;
make it plain on tablets, so he may run who reads it.
—Habakkuk 2:2

Coincidentally, when we finally arrived on the Island of Lésvos, it was World Refugee Day. I didn't even know such a thing existed. After we attended a training session for the camp where we would serve, we went to a program at the ruins of an ancient castle. This was my first time in Europe, and I was excited to see a castle. However, I had no idea what the program really was.

As we entered the path leading to the castle ruins, there were refugee women, draped with beautiful headscarves, telling stories of their journeys to that point. Many gathered around, listening intently to them – and the interpreters. They were soft spoken, appearing somewhat shy, yet they bravely stood and spoke. Tables with supplies for writing notes lined a path leading to a grove of trees.

Refugees and aid workers were writing notes on strips of rubber left from the many boats and rafts that brought the refugees to this island. Then, they were hanging them on the trees. A note tied around a large tree trunk explained the vision of this event. It said the following: "The Solidarity Tree: An initiative by the shoreline response teams and independent volunteers of Camp Fire, to respectfully honor those who passed through Lésvos on the journey to a better and safer future. World Refugee Day 6/20/2016."

I could not keep the tears from streaming as I read the words so carefully written on the strips:

"I wish to have a joyful life and I hope the UN finds a solution for us."

"I want life. I want to be alive. I wish to open a door of peace on our face."

"I wish to reach my destination, and for all the refugees, I pray to God that the tears on my face will dry."

There were hundreds of notes, each tied to beautiful trees with bright red and blue ribbons. Although written in multiple languages, each note had the same theme: They missed home; they wanted peace; they wanted to leave this island; they wanted to find their family members; and they wanted to *hope* again!

Volunteers from all over the island had come together. Many were sharing stories of rescues at sea, others helped on the beaches or at reception centers. Many gave clothes or food. Others helped with the massive transportation issues from one end of the island to the other. There was also the daily cycle of hours of beach clean-up. I believe this event was not only for the refugees but for the volunteers and the residents, as well. This was a way to process experiences they shared with each other. Only those exhausted inhabitants on the island could truly understand the magnitude of the crisis forming here.

Later that week, we visited a trash dump and saw with our own eyes the mountains of life vests, rafts, and boats which a half a million people left behind after they landed on this small island. Each item had a story, an adventure, or a tragedy to tell. The dump felt like a graveyard, very different than walking under the canopy of trees I had experienced a few days earlier. It was the graveyard of a previous lifestyle.

The island was full of beauty: beaches, castles, quaint shops, and even a petrified forest! It was also full of kind, tired, and frustrated people. Life had not only changed for the new inhabitants but for the longtime residents as well.

 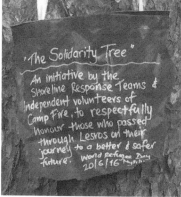

For your reference, the following are a few statistics that represent this time in history from the UNHCR office of Lésvos (www.unhcr.org):

- 2015: 431,989 documented refugees landed on Lésvos.
- 2016: 91,506 documented refugees landed on Lésvos.
- 2017: 12,795 documented refugees landed on Lésvos.
- 2018: 15,034 documented refugees landed on Lésvos

And the numbers are still climbing.

Facts about Lésvos:

- Lésvos (or Lésbos) is sometimes referred to as Mytilene, the name of its capital city. This island of 631 square miles is the third largest island in the Aegean Sea, with 199 miles of coastline (National Statistics Service of Greece).
- Some 86,000 people lived here before the refugees began arriving (NSSG).
- Lesbos lies in the far east of the Aegean Sea, facing the Turkish coast—the gulf of Edremit—from the north and east.
- Lesbos is 164.3 miles (142.68 nautical miles) from Athens.
- At one point, there are only six miles of ocean between Lésvos and the coast of Turkey, making it one of the narrowest waterways between Turkey and the European Union.

Scriptures for Refugee Care

"When a stranger sojourns with you in your land, you shall
not do him wrong. You shall treat the stranger who sojourns
with you as the native among you, and you shall love him as
yourself, for you were strangers in the land of Egypt: I am the
Lord your God." —Leviticus 19:33-34

"When you reap the harvest of your land, you shall not reap
your field right up to its edge, neither shall you gather the
gleanings after your harvest. And you shall not strip your
vineyard bare, neither shall you gather the fallen grapes of
your vineyard. You shall leave them for the poor and for the
sojourner: I am the Lord your God." —Leviticus 19:9-10

"He executes justice for the fatherless and the widow, and
loves the sojourner, giving him food and clothing. Love the
sojourner, therefore, for you were sojourners in the land of
Egypt." —Deuteronomy 10:18-19

"Behold, this was the guilt of your sister Sodom: she and her
daughters had pride, excess of food, and prosperous ease, but
did not aid the poor and needy." —Ezekiel 16:49

"You shall not oppress a sojourner. You know the heart of a
sojourner, for you were sojourners in the land of Egypt."
—Exodus 23:9

"The sojourner has not lodged in the street; I have opened
my doors to the traveler." —Job 31:32

"Then I will draw near to you for judgment. I will be a swift witness against the sorcerers, against the adulterers, against those who swear falsely, against those who oppress the hired worker in his wages, the widow and the fatherless, against those who thrust aside the sojourner, and do not fear me, says the Lord of hosts." —Malachi 3:5

"For I was hungry and you gave me food, I was thirsty and you gave me drink, I was a stranger and you welcomed me, I was naked and you clothed me, I was sick and you visited me, I was in prison and you came to me." —Matthew 25:35-36

"For just as the body is one and has many members, and all the members of the body, though many, are one body, so it is with Christ. For in one Spirit we were all baptized into one body—Jews or Greeks, slaves or free—and all were made to drink of one Spirit. For the body does not consist of one member but of many." —1 Corinthians 12:12-14

"For the whole law is fulfilled in one word: 'You shall love your neighbor as yourself.'" —Galatians 5:14

"But he, desiring to justify himself, said to Jesus, 'And who is my neighbor?' Jesus replied, 'A man was going down from Jerusalem to Jericho, and he fell among robbers, who stripped him and beat him and departed, leaving him half dead. Now by chance a priest was going down that road, and when he saw him he passed by on the other side. So likewise a Levite, when he came to the place and saw him, passed by on the other side. But a Samaritan, as he journeyed, came to where he was, and when he saw him, he had compassion. He went to him and bound up his wounds, pouring on oil and wine. Then he set him on his own animal and brought him to an inn and took care of him. And the next day he took out two denarii and gave them to the innkeeper, saying, "Take care of him, and whatever more you spend, I will repay you when I come back." Which of these three, do you think, proved to be a neighbor to the man who fell among the robbers?' He said, 'The one who showed him mercy.' And Jesus said to him, 'You go, and do likewise.'"

—Luke 10:29-37

Chapter 5

The Girl in the Pink-Striped Dress

"For I was hungry and you gave me food, I was thirsty and you gave me drink, I was a stranger and you welcomed me, I was naked and you clothed me, I was sick and you visited me, I was in prison and you came to me."
—Matthew 25:35-36

My senses were trying to take in what I was seeing as we entered Camp Moria. Someone had just given us official lanyards that allowed us to come and go. We put on vests that identified us as volunteers. We were directed to the evacuation routes, just in case. No photos were permitted, but the images are etched in my mind forever.

The camp is built on a hillside. A perfect hill to ride a sled or whiz down on a bike, but none of that could happen here. It was hot and extremely crowded. Makeshift tents stood between former military barracks and storage containers. This was summer 2016, and about 4,000 people were living in a space designed for 900. I'd like to be able to say that is no longer the case, but when I returned in summer 2018, there were more than 7,000 people living there.

The "residents" did not have lanyards. At that time, they

were being detained and could not come and go freely. (This policy has since been changed.) What was supposed to be a processing center—a quick stop on their way to building a new life as they traveled to a place of safety—was instead where they would live for months at a time, unsure of when they would be able to leave. This was not what they had anticipated.

They were trapped in a camp that was trapped on an island. Even if they left the camp, they would still have to arrange a flight or ferry passage to Athens. Again, this was nearly impossible without being properly processed, so they waited in the camp for their next assignment. Where would they go next? Who would allow them in?

We arrived when the European borders closed. Neighboring countries were overwhelmed. Greece—and, in this case, the island of Lésvos—was doing the best it could with the large number of daily arrivals. It was an impossible task.

Many non-governmental organizations had pulled out of the area as an act of protest against detainment. Those left were from all over the globe, young and old. Their tasks were basic: boat rescues, shelter, food, and clothing. They tried to provide items for basic dignity. These were simple, yet extremely significant tasks.

The volunteers themselves had chosen to leave the comforts of home to make others a tad more comfortable in extremely uncomfortable conditions. Some gave up permanent jobs and moved their families to this island to serve. Others gave up a summer. All of them made financial sacrifices. They looked so tired. The camp was extremely understaffed. Some staff looked shell-shocked, as if they had been in a battle. Still, there was laughter, and hugs, too. Many times I shake my head at the evil I see, but I choose to believe that at that moment, I served with angels.

Those in charge had only been there a few months. I eagerly greeted my partner and guide for the day. She was in her early twenties, from Pennsylvania.

"How long have you been here?" I asked.

"I just started yesterday!" she replied, surprising me. But she seemed to have a good working knowledge of the camp, its routine, and its various sections. I was even more surprised to learn that the next day, I would be a guide!

A void of hope quickly became evident. Despair filled the air. It was palpable. Irritation was everywhere. The authorities turned the water on only twice a day. People were aggravated with each other. The day consisted of standing in line for food, for clothing, for showers. The children didn't have a school. Before arriving on Lésvos, they lived in comfortable homes with electricity and running water; they had cell phones and cars and went to restaurants and gathered with family. They attended school and played music and games. Their lives *were* a lot like the volunteers' lives but ... no longer.

On our first afternoon, we served food. I met a sweet little girl in a pink-and-white-striped dress. She was probably around ten years old, very petite, and had dark curly hair. She was in line to receive food. The metal take-out containers were very hot. We were trying to show the children how to carry the containers from the rim rather than holding the bottom, so they would not burn their hands. Not one person dropped their food container, even when they held it the wrong way. I know their hands had to be burning, but the food was too precious to lose.

The little girl repeatedly stood in line, and when her turn

came, we repeatedly gave her food. I watched her joyfully run with the container each time. I joked with her about her "home delivery service." She eventually came back, but this time not wanting more food but wanting to help. She started putting plastic forks in each container. We ended up with a small group of young helpers who easily found their way to our side of a flimsy makeshift barrier, but she stood out to me.

Then there was the group of children begging for extra salt. Instead of sprinkling the teaspoon of salt on their pasta, they wanted it in their hands. They popped that teaspoon of salt into their mouths and savored it like it was sugar. I think their little bodies were craving salt because of the dehydrating effect of the 100° daily temperatures.

The next day we returned to distribute shoes. My section was near the entrance and close to where we had set up to hand out food the night before. I was delighted when about halfway into my route, the girl in the pink-and-white-striped dress greeted me. She grew excited as we approached her makeshift tent. Our task was to measure the children's feet, make a list, and return to fit the children with new shoes. When we got to her tent, she eagerly motioned us in. It was hot and dim. It was *full* of women and children. I now saw where she was taking all those meals and understood how she was helping so everyone didn't have to wait in line.

We measured feet and returned with the shoes. They all knew the English words, *Thank you.* The little girl walked with us like a guide, enjoying her new shoes as we made a few other deliveries.

Two days later, I was back. Our group was easy to spot in our orange shirts. The little girl greeted us, still wearing the pink-and-white-striped dress after four 100° days in dusty and dirty surroundings. However, the dress was not noticeably dirty, and I wondered if her mother found a way to wash it each night. Did she wear this dress as she fled her country, while the bombs landed close to her family? Did she arrive in this dress? She had to have arrived on this island on a crowded raft or boat. Many of the stories of the crossing are quite traumatic. Or did she receive it with a dress voucher when she arrived at the camp? Either way, she had been wearing the same sweet dress for at least four days.

On that particular day, we couldn't spend much time with her, because we were working in another area of the camp. She walked with us as far as she could, staying in her basic section of the camp. I think I will always remember the image of this sweet little girl—not fully knowing her story but completely understanding that it is a traumatic one. I am reminded to pray for her every time I see a little girl in a pink-and-white-striped dress.

I also remember her because she was one of the few positive lights in this very harsh environment. My daughter saw a body wrapped in a rug and carried out. A fight broke out in a group of young men. We heard the angry requests for clothes and basic supplies.

We heard no music, or singing, or laughter. Yes, we heard, "Thank you." But we saw only hopelessness.

I turned my thoughts from the little girl. I was pleased to meet my interpreter for the day. He, too, lived at the camp.

"Thank you so much for helping me today," I said.

"Oh, it is my pleasure," he replied. As we visited the various tents, gathering the needed shoe sizes, we continued our conversation. "How old are you?" I asked. He was twenty-eight. "How did you learn English so well?"

"I worked with many Americans at my job with Exxon,"

he explained. "Several of my friends there actually gave me money for my journey."

I asked if he'd come alone, and he said that he'd traveled with his brother and sister-in-law. I assumed that he must be anxious to leave the camp.

"I have already obtained my official papers giving me passage to Athens," he said. In Athens, he would receive further instructions and clearance to travel to Germany. But he surprised me when he declared: "I will not leave here until my brother and sister-in-law also receive their papers. I cannot leave them." He had no idea how long that wait would be.

A precious grandmother begged me for shoes for her grandbabies. I thought of my grandchildren and knew I would do the same. At first, it struck me how many refugees had cell phones, despite their utter poverty, but cell phones were the lifelines to finding family members who had settled elsewhere. Many families had been separated along their exodus from home. Facebook helped them to reconnect. Even if they still had some savings left, they simply could not purchase a plane ticket without a visa or passport. Many of the refugees were professional people—homeowners and shopkeepers—but now they were stuck, and their resources were dwindling.

I heard stories of loved ones lost when their homes were bombed and others lost as they fled their homes. We weren't permitted to say very much, and we couldn't offer prayer. I understood this request, and we abided by it, because the wrong conversation could ignite offense, arguments, or worse. Still, it grieved me, because I had no way to offer the Hope that they needed. I could only remember them in my prayers and remind myself that the story was not finished.

On many previous trips, when we left an orphanage or church, we would hug the people we had served and maybe exchange Facebook information. Children would play and sing. It often felt as if we were leaving lifelong friends. My departure from Moria was quite different.

Within the detainment area was a detainment center. Basically, it was a jail for those who had made threats, gotten into fights, or worse. Officials decided that these individuals could not wander freely through the camp, and we did not enter this area. It was too dangerous. The detainees were simply behind a fence near the entrance where our group gathered to depart. They could easily look out at us. One day, my back was to the fence, along with several other team members. A colleague was facing me, and I could tell immediately that something was wrong.

"Don't turn around," he said, "Don't look!"

A young man behind the fence had clasped his hands together, extended his pointer finger to mimic a gun, taken a stance, and begun to pretend to shoot us one by one by one.

We were there to help. Did we do any good? Did we make any difference?

During the trip, we stayed with Aphrodite at her beautiful Aphrodite Hotel in Molyvos. We came after Anderson Cooper, CNN, and many other news institutions arrived. While we served at the camp, Gina and a few others stayed with team members who were minors. Together, they cleaned beaches and helped to host fun events for the local children. They also organized the mounds of supplies that had been sent from all over the globe. We did several other projects, too.

We also shopped. Yes, we called it the "shopping ministry." Many of the business owners were struggling. This was a tourist area normally, but who wants to vacation at a beach where hundreds of refugees are arriving on its shores daily? The businesses were barely able to stay open, so team members were very deliberate about shopping for their Christmas season gifts and taking them home to the United States. Joy lit up the shop owners' faces. Some shop owners even called Aphrodite to thank her for sending the shoppers.

Aphrodite told us many stories. She once welcomed a boat of former professional musicians. The next day they returned to thank her and give her one of their CDs. However, she didn't recognize them, so much had a shower and some dry clothing changed their appearance. Another time, an older man was resting on one of the beach chairs. As he got up, he dropped his keys. When Aphrodite's father pointed out the keys, he replied, "I left them on purpose. They belong to a home I no longer have."

Strangers from all over the world began sending Aphrodite boxes of clothes and supplies. The boxes filled an entire hotel room. Media outlets showed up and stayed at her hotel: CNN, BBC, ABC, and others. Anderson Cooper was just one of the journalists who interviewed her.

Aphrodite recalls lying in bed and hearing the boats land in the wee hours of the morning. Many times, they got up to help, but they were exhausted. The arrivals were not stopping. Eventually, the family made signs with pictures, pointing people to bins with dry clothing and blankets. The bins had once housed pool toys, but now the family created a makeshift waiting area with their pool furniture. Arrivals could gather there until Aphrodite got her children ready for school. Then, she would make the needed calls to arrange for transportation to the processing center for yet another group. When the people were too many to transport, after a period of rest and a snack, the arrivals would proceed by foot. Aphrodite's family then began the arduous task of cleaning their beach, hoping their paying guests would not check out but continue their vacations. Aphrodite made sure to stop in time to pick up her children from school, and then in the afternoon she worked as a tutor. She was trying to keep life "normal," but it was far from it.

We prayed for the Greek people. We prayed for the refugees. We especially prayed for the people of Lésvos. We danced to Greek music and ate fantastic food.

But, deep down, I was grieved. The time in the camp affected me more than I had realized. We focused on our acts of kindness, but were they enough?

I couldn't sleep. I had to process—but I had no time for it, because Botswana was calling!

Chapter 6

Lions and Elephants and Hippos! Oh, My!

Who comforts us in all our affliction, so that we may be able to comfort those who are in any affliction, with the comfort with which we ourselves are comforted by God.
—2 Corinthians 1:4

I had been to several countries in Africa but never to Botswana. I was going with a small team on an exploratory trip. My host was a missionary friend whom I had served with in Kyrgyzstan, and I was looking forward to the reunion.

We were the guests of a safari company foundation. I enjoy safaris. I love elephants, and there is nothing like seeing them in the wild, as well as lions, giraffes, zebras, and hippos. So, although we were on a mission trip, I was looking forward to enjoying several game rides.

When we arrived at the camp, an electric gate opened to welcome us into the compound. While it was not as large or as grand, it reminded me of the doors in the Jurassic Park movie. A wall and electric wire enclosed the small compound. These kept the lions, elephants, and other wild animals from invading the space. However, every day, when we exited that compound and visited with the people living in the village, I saw as many wild animals driving from hut to hut as I saw on safari. It was surreal.

The locals lived in huts built with bricks made from termite mounds. A few cinder block homes were sprinkled in. Most huts did not have doors, because no opening was made to a standard size. Unlike the compound where I was sleeping, there wasn't a compound wall or a door to protect the people from wild animals at night. No one there walks around after dusk, because this is in the middle of the *Okavango Delta*. The wild dogs, hyenas, leopards, hippos, elephants, and lions are all on the move. Many families keep dogs as "pets," knowing a lion will grab the dog before grabbing their child. Please don't judge them. I love my pet, but I would sacrifice it in a skinny minute for my child!

The Bush Ways Foundation provided doors for the huts. For just $30 a door, everyone would be able to sleep safe and sound. It was a joy when I was able to send a Samaritan's Feet team back to partner with the foundation to help build some doors. I love learning of a tangible need, then making arrangements to supply it. If only all projects could be as cut and dry as providing and hanging a door.

That doesn't mean it didn't take some effort. Remember, no entryway was the same size, there is no local hardware store, and the team had to bring tools, and, oh, yeah ... people had to raise funds, not only for the supplies but also for expensive plane tickets.

On my visit, I made arrangements to serve a large group of teen moms at a community center. The workshop explained to the young women how their bodies worked. We had beautiful feminine hygiene products from Days for Girls. I also had a huge variety of sports bras from an organization called Supporting the Girls, and each came with inspirational notes. In addition, they received new shoes and socks from Samaritan's Feet. It felt like Christmas.

It was a joy to visit the various huts and fit the families with new shoes, as well as offer additional supplies and prayer. It was fun giving lots of hugs and making new friends.

The food was good; the accommodations were lovely; and my team was low-maintenance, enjoyable, and easy. Of course, it was also hot—over 100° every day—and there wasn't any air-conditioning. I had never drunk so much water and other liquids in one day in my life.

Finally, I had a break from the last several months of hard, gut-wrenching trips. Except …

Botswana had passed a law requiring all children to attend school. I am a big supporter of education. With every fiber, I believe that education is the key to escaping poverty. It unlocks so many opportunities. It seems like this law would be fantastic, but the implementation of that law was chilling.

Instead of the government building schools in the villages for the children to attend, they were transporting the children to a government school that was more than a hundred miles away. The children in this community were sent to a school that was a three-hour drive away from their homes. Children as young as five were loaded—standing room only—in the back of a truck. Children who had *never* left their villages were now being sent to a government boarding school. I can only imagine how afraid they must have been.

To some degree, the parents were happy that their children were going to get an education—something they'd never had the chance to receive. But they missed their children. They didn't have cars. They had no way to check on their children or visit them. The children were permitted to come home for two visits and for summer break.

These parents did not see what we had seen. They did not understand what we now understood about their children's well-being, because we had visited this school. We weren't allowed to take photos. The staff knew we were coming, and I'm sure they prepared for our visit. It was clean, but it was sparse, very sparse. Local children also attended this school.

The village children lived in dorms. This "boarding school" had forty children to one dorm room caregiver. The caregiver wasn't required to sleep in the same room with the children. Each child was assigned to a bunk bed, but some children had to sleep together, because there weren't enough beds. There were several dorm rooms. We noticed security fencing around the caregiver's home on the property, but there was no security on the school property. From what we gathered, locals could easily access the children. A colleague on my team specializes in children with trauma, and she quickly identified several concerns: older children, younger children—very vulnerable children with no protection.

There were very minimal provisions. I did not see one toy. No child had a locker or any personal items. School uniforms were tattered and torn. In fact, I was struck at the tattered and unkempt condition of their clothing. I then learned that all ages, even the five-year-old students, were required to wash and care for their own clothing.

We had brought a special lunch for the children. Along with sandwiches, we had chips, fruit, and cookies. The children quickly lined up, almost like robots. There wasn't much talking and little laughter or interaction with each other. In layman's terms, they simply seemed shell-shocked. They were polite, and they thanked us for the food before quietly finding a place to sit and eat. Almost all of them ate the fruit first, not the cookie. The fruit was a special treat.

I've been in many schools, some with much greater poverty. The schools I'd seen in refugee camps in Uganda had more poverty, but they also had laughter and singing. This school was missing joy. Maybe the situation improved over time. I hope so.

We had planned to give new shoes to the children who were from the village we had visited. However, we quickly realized that this wasn't possible. We didn't think they would be able to keep the shoes. Instead, we decided to give shoes to their parents to present to them on their next visit home. We left this experience heavyhearted. What could we do?

I returned home, and I thought about my last several months. When I closed my eyes, scenes flashed in my mind. I could see the burn marks on the ground and the bruises on the arms of the beaten refugees in Morocco. I couldn't shake the hopelessness of the refugees in Camp Moria in Greece. I shuddered and pushed away the memory of the young man behind the fence pretending to shoot us with his clasped hands … one by one by one. I vividly remembered the burning of the hot food I had scooped into tender hands.

I can still feel the body of a starving little girl I held in my arms. I wonder if she and her sister are still alive. I think of a small, five-year-old child in tattered clothing trapped in a vulnerable situation at a boarding school, hundreds of miles from the safety of his termite-brick hut. And so, after my journeys begins my own journey—my journey for answers.

But Jesus said, "Let the little children come to me and do not hinder them, for to such belongs the kingdom of heaven."
—Matthew 19:14

A termite mound!

A hut that needed a door

Chapter 7

However, I Am Anxious

*Say to those who have an anxious heart, "Be strong; fear not! Behold, your God will come with vengeance, with the recompense of God. He will come and save you." —*Isaiah 35:4

There is not much down time in my life. It always amazes me after incredible journeys how quickly I slide back into daily life. About a week later, a trip can become a distant memory. I usually have one day—generally, the first day back in the office—when I just want to quit. I have no idea why, as I love my job. Because I know this about myself, I've just learned to ignore those feelings when they come. I recognize the glazed look on the faces of friends and family as I attempt to show photos of my last journey. It reminds me of a time when I was a kid going to a family friend's home and watching a slide show (remember those?!) of their family's Grand Canyon trip ... that went on and on. Boring! I do not want to be *that* person, but I think I often am! I try not to talk about it too much, although I am sure my immediate family may disagree. I try to pick and share only the top ten photos.

Also, I realize that when I return it's hard for my family, co-workers, and friends to understand my passion or my feelings. I think it is hard for anyone to truly understand another person's firsthand experiences.

For example, my family all played sports, but I was always the *mercy pick* in gym class! Often, the only reason I wasn't picked last was because a friend had *mercy* on me and let me join their team. When the other team would shout, "Hit it to the hole!" the ball always came my way. I was "the hole."

My husband, Greg, played semi-pro football. I attended most of his games and was his personal cheerleader. Yet, I truly never understood what it was like to be hit by a 300-pound man, have your body ache for days, and still desire to do it all again.

My daughter, Alysse, was an all-conference volleyball player in high school. She continued to play in college and then coached volleyball when she became a teacher. She also played four years of high school basketball and three years of soccer. During a basketball game in eighth grade, she overextended and tore several ligaments in her right ankle. Immediately, she fell on the floor, crying in pain. I cried just watching her cry. Greg quickly scooped her up, and off to the emergency room we went. Months of braces and physical therapy ensued. With my great love of team sports, I would have called it quits, but Alysse's experience was different. She loved playing sports and being a part of a team. She did the therapy needed to work through the pain and continue to participate in the sports she loved.

My mind is always on the next thing, and I don't take much time to process the past. I think this is common for many people. But this time, I was finding, the past insisted on being heard. I didn't have a torn ligament, but I did need to work through my pain so I could effectively continue to serve in the areas that I loved. My pain wasn't as obvious as my daughter's as she cried out on the basketball court. It revealed itself in quiet tears at night that trickled softly down my cheeks while I made sure to face away from my husband and hide the turmoil that was taking me by surprise. Why was this return so different? After so many journeys, over so many years, why now was I unable to trust God in the circumstances that I had seen?

I was anxious. I had never had much anxiety in the past, but it was now a daily companion. I counted my blessings, and I was grateful. I spent time with my beautiful family. I lived in a lovely home. I didn't have to worry about how I was going to pay my bills or where my next meal would come from. I felt safe. Why was I anxious? I could easily repeat God's word:

"Do not be anxious about anything, but in everything by prayer and supplication with thanksgiving let your requests be made known to God" (Philippians 4:6).

I was still anxious. And while I completely believe in the power of God's Word—in fact my life is totally built on my belief in the scriptures—those scriptures are not a "magic spell." If it was only as easy as Harry Potter shouting his spell, *"Expecto Patronum!"* and poof! Harry is automatically protected.

I did all the things I usually do: I spend time with my sweet friends and co-workers; I eat out—a lot; I shop when I want to, get my nails done and color my hair; I go to church and to my Bible study; I indulge my grandchildren and spend time at my oceanfront condo. My life is blessed.

However, this time, I was anxious, almost fretting.

I also worked hard. I put in very long days. I liked my job. It was rewarding. Still, I was anxious, fretting, and exhausted.

I couldn't push the feelings away. I grieved. I prayed. And then I asked, "Why? Why, God, have you allowed me to see this? What is required of me? What can I do? There is so much I can do nothing about. I cannot fix it. I cannot sleep. I feel paralyzed."

I am anxious, fretting, exhausted ... and paralyzed.

I had done my devotions, some days. I had read Scripture, some days. I had spent time in prayer every day. But now I had reached the point where I needed to hear specific answers from God. I looked to God's Word, as it must have an answer. I don't know why I hadn't desperately searched His Word weeks ago, because I am so grateful for His mercy to help in our time of need (Hebrews 4:16). But now I was ready. I was ready to stop fretting. I was ready to find my why ... and what would be required of me.

I have read Psalm 37 many times. In the past, I had mainly concentrated on the much-quoted verses four and five: "Delight yourself in the Lord, and he will give you the desires of your heart. Commit your way to the Lord; trust in him, and he will act" (Psalm 37:4-5).

This time, however, the preceding verses leapt off of the page, and I clung to them. These verses gave me the answer to "What now?" I hope these verses will speak to you, too:

"Fret not yourself because of evildoers; be not envious of wrongdoers! For they will soon fade like the grass and wither like the green herb. Trust in the Lord, and do good; dwell in the land and befriend faithfulness" (Psalm 37:1-3).

This verse gave me five instructions:

1. Stop fretting.
2. Trust in the Lord.
3. Do good.
4. Dwell in your land.
5. Befriend faithfulness.

I like instructions; I need actions. I could do this!

Chapter 8

Stop Fretting

Fret not yourself because of evil doers; be not envious of wrongdoers!
For they will soon fade like the grass and wither like the green herb.
—Psalm 37:1-2

The world had become a different place. I was not the only one fretting. Every place I looked, people were fretting. The 2016 United States election was in full swing. The dialogue was horrible, and many were fretting about the state of our elected officials. There was fretting over the refugee crisis, over opening and closing borders, over gun control. Some wanted more guns to combat the violent people, and others wanted to restrict guns to disarm violent people. People were fretting over the weather, hurricanes, and wild fires. There are so many reasons to fret:

A mad man shoots at an innocent crowd in Las Vegas.
A terrorist drives his truck onto a crowded street.
Americans have seen one school shooting after another.
Women reveal experiences with harassment.
Children testify of abuse.
Racial tensions have increased.

There is so much evil that we can do very little to prevent. I have always been an optimist. It has been easy for me to believe that people are good; we can work hard, and make a difference. However, deep in my core, I was no longer sure. I believe that is what the enemy of our soul, Satan, wants us to do, to be paralyzed, to give up. We can become so overwhelmed by the evil that we replace action with fretting.

Then I read this verse that tells me not to fret because of the evildoers. God will take care of them. My anxiousness, my fretting, my paralyzed state does not help.

I got a glimpse of eternity.

My children have made fun of me for what I'm about to describe. I have a 100th birthday box. It is decorated and lives on the top shelf of my closet. Inside it, I place special cards or little mementos to mark memorable experiences or meaningful friendships. I have told my children that on my 100th birthday, they are to decorate my room with the items in this box. Then, we will gather the family: my children, grandchildren, and great grandchildren. They will read the notes, and through this celebration be reminded of the joy and love and faithfulness of God to our family.

"Oh, Mom! Do you really think you are going to live to be 100?" they ask. Well, yes, I know I will. I know because I am an eternal being. I will be alive someplace. I'm not sure if my home will still be here on earth or in glory—but make no mistake, I will still be alive! So, open that box on my hundredth birthday, because I know that "whoever believes in him may have eternal life. For God so loved the world, that he gave his only Son, that whoever believes in him should not perish but have eternal life" (John 3:15-16).

When we look at life through the filter of eternity, it does make it easier not to fret about all the evil around us. It will wither and fade, and God will execute his justice.

Since the fall of man, evil has always been. The Bible is full of evildoers and wrongdoers. All of the disciples, except for John, were martyred for their faith. They were holy men, doing God's will. However, they understood that this earth was not their permanent home. I think they had a glimpse of eternity.

While he was in prison, the Apostle Paul wrote, "For to me to live is Christ, and to die is gain" (Philippians 1:21). While we may suffer for a time here, we must keep our faith and knowledge that when we have a hope in Jesus, it really is a short time in comparison to eternity. I will gain glimpses of eternity in some difficult situations to come. And when I can grasp it—even for a short time—it brings such peace.

I have returned to Athens, Greece, three times since that first visit, and to Lésvos, specifically, once. I am currently preparing for a fourth visit.

While in Athens, I served at a refugee help center. In addition to the help center, I visited two camps, as well as a boarding home for refugees. All were much better than Moria, although none were close to the standard of living most of the refugees had before. But each place had a sense of community. The children could attend school. Families generally had a bedroom to share. I witnessed a lot of gratefulness here. Even so, there was a natural mourning for what was lost and a fear of the unknown future.

I was at the ministry home when a family of five arrived. They looked so tired. They were quiet and gracious. There was already twenty-three people living in this single-family home. The teen girls who lived there quickly served us all hot tea. I had come to work, not to be served. However, I simply said thank you and took the time to have a cup of hot tea or two. Sometimes, I get caught up in being efficient with a task and miss out on the relationship of the moment, but I slowed down that day.

The tired family waited patiently as we cleared a former storage room, their soon-to-be new home. No one could predict for how long. I then sat down to sip the hot tea with them. I tried to communicate, and with a little help from the son who spoke broken English, we were actually doing quite well. I showed photos of my family members, and they told me about their former home.

The father was very expressive in making sure that I knew that he was a graduate of the University of Bulgaria. He had worked as an electrical engineer and had been a good provider for his family. Now this family from Syria would share a small bedroom and live in a home with twenty-three strangers. As we left, I asked for permission to pray with them. They willingly accepted. It was all I could do. I will continue to pray for this sweet family, and many others like them. It is what I must now do.

When the week ended, my team returned to the United Sates, and I continued on to Lésvos to revisit Camp Moria. I wanted to explore future opportunities and see how to best help. I was neither excited about nor dreading the next few days of service. I was not afraid at all, but I was very aware of everything around me. My focus had changed from leading to learning as my location changed from Athens to Lésvos. I knew there was a purpose to this visit for now and for the future. I had connected with some great teachers and servants on my first trip, and I hoped that there would be positive changes compared to two years ago.

I would love to report that Camp Moria was much better, that hope had returned! But there were now 7,000 people living in that same space designed for 900. There were more tents than the last time. When a family was relocated, the camp sent a volunteer to simply sit in the tent and keep others from taking the space. I stopped and spoke with a young Mennonite girl from Pennsylvania who had this role. Several new arrivals were in a large community barracks tent, and the next family on the waiting list would be relocated to the newly vacated tent.

My heart ached as I sat in a small tent with a mom and four daughters. They trembled as another volunteer and I held their hands. They told us that the eldest daughter had been raped on the journey. Tears flowed from all of our eyes. The daughter could not sleep; she was too frightened. This insomnia caused her to act irrationally. All I could do was listen and assure her that nothing was her fault. My colleague, a lawyer, was going to try to get the girl moved to a women-only-area where she could sleep. The family knew we were Christians. I told the girl that I would pray for her, not in a trite way, but in a very fervent way. It was all I could do, and she wanted that prayer. I prayed.

During my first visit to Moria, no prayer was permitted. In my later visit, the camp was peppered with prayer; respectfully and privately inside tents—never forced, only when asked. The praying, while not in the open, was certainly happening daily and often. I received the following report back from my most recent visit. I have edited the letter to a few bullet points and have changed the names, but I want to encourage you with the eternal difference that is being made:

- We know of five Muslims who have accepted Christ as their savior.

- Around thirty to forty others received electronic Bibles or New Testaments. Many have indicated to us that they are reading God's Word in Moria Refugee Camp.

- We also have had the joy of discipling some of the followers of Isa (Jesus).

- Pray for A, who is continuing to grow in the Lord and remains faithful. (My friend was able to have a phone call with him about some issues he is facing.)

- Pray for B who is still reading his Bible but has not yet received God's salvation.

- Pray for young C and for D and family, who are ministering to him.

- Pray for E, who has embraced Christ and is hungry for fellowship but reluctant to go to church for fear of persecution.

- Pray for F and family, that they would seek Christ.

This work is hard, and I do pray often for those doing it full-time, because the highs and lows of the situation are exhausting. In my brief time in Moria, I felt some of that, myself. One example of that is what happened when I left the camp on my last trip.

I had made arrangements with a specific driver to pick me up and take me to the airport. This was after the emotional experience in the tent that I talked about earlier, as well as several other conversations with new arrivals. I was physically and emotionally exhausted. There is a trench with grates that surrounds the camp. It runs downhill and carries sewage away from the camp.

I was at the entrance, at the bottom of the hill. I stepped on to a grate, and … yep, it broke. I found myself alone with a twisted ankle and standing in sewage up to my knees. As I looked up, I saw my driver. In my mind, I'm begging him not to leave me. He had compassion and let me enter his very clean car.

I literally got to the airport in time to check in and board my flight from the island to Athens. Yes, I was still wearing the same clothes. No one spoke to me. Honestly, *I* didn't even want to be with me! It seemed like a fitting end to a hard day. Pardon my pun, but I felt crappy on the inside and looked like crap on the outside—literally. But my day was not over. Once I got to my hotel room in Athens, I threw those pants away! I took a *long* shower and even used hand sanitizer on my legs. Then, I ordered room service and enjoyed the nice, clean sheets and comfortable bed. It was heavenly. I don't think I would have appreciated that beautiful room nearly as much if I had not just stepped up to my knees in sewage.

Please understand what I am saying. I do not want to lessen the trauma in any way, but if we have trauma here on earth, but then we have eternity with the Lord, then we can fret the evil we see on earth much less. I believe that God created man with a free will: the decision to do good or the decision to do evil. Those decisions always have repercussions on others. It's the result of living in a fallen world, a world that chooses sin over righteousness.

In my own immediate family I had one family member experience rape; my husband lost both parents to cancer; and my father was tragically killed in a car accident. Why didn't God intervene with a different outcome? I don't know. I wish He had. I have seen God do miracles. I have experienced His protection in my own car accident. Why was I unharmed and my father died? I believe that my father and my in-laws are rejoicing in heaven. I have seen my family member who was raped go on to serve God faithfully for many years, not letting that trauma define her but going on to live an abundant life. God gave her the strength she needed through the power of the Holy Spirit. I don't understand it. I choose to accept the sovereignty of God *by faith*. It is not easy. Without *faith* it is impossible.

What if this refugee migration brings many people into contact with Christians and their lives are altered for eternity? We must remember that for believers the day is coming when those ruined garments will be tossed, and we will be sanitized and comforted and it will be heavenly. It *will be* heaven. However, just because I have a glimpse of eternity, because I am able to "fret" less, does that mean that then I do nothing? Of course not! Psalm 37 does not stop there. We move on to the four instructions of what we can do and what I believe helps to combat the fretting!

Visiting the warehouse for Camp Moria

Chapter 9

Trust in the Lord!

Trust in the Lord, and do good;
dwell in the land and befriend faithfulness.
—Psalm 37:3

The first "do" on my list is to *trust* in the Lord. It sounds so basic—and it is. However, it is a must if we are going to find peace as we maneuver through this complicated life. I was privileged to come to salvation at age twelve. One Sunday night at the altar in a small Nazarene Church in Ohio, I prayed to accept Jesus. I confessed my sins and very sincerely asked Jesus to be the Lord of my life. While I certainly did not walk in perfection from that point on, I always felt His presence with me. I have had many examples in my life of answered prayers and evidence of God at work. I have included some examples of his miracles and His voice speaking to me in the back of this book. Those experiences, along with many others, have built my faith to be able to trust in the Lord.

I knew I could *trust* the Lord.

I know it can be a struggle, but I am blessed that this part does come easy for me—easier than the "not fretting" in the previous chapter. If I can trust the Lord in my personal life, I must *trust* that He is at work in the lives of others that I meet, even those in the most difficult of circumstances, including the ones that were causing me to fret and lose sleep at night.

I'll never forget an unscheduled stop as we left a refugee camp in Uganda. This new camp had mud huts sprinkled throughout the massive landscape. Our team had just participated in distributing shoes and helping with a feeding program at a school in the camp. We had a little time to interact with the children as we gathered our supplies to head to the next camp. The children gathered around us as we were loading into our van. My brother was holding a speaker on his shoulders, blaring fun kids' songs. He reminded me of the cool kid in the 70s with the big boom box, walking down the street. He was dancing, the kids were dancing, and though we were surrounded with poverty, at that moment we were also surrounded with joy. As we prepared to depart, the children followed him to our van as if he were the Pied Piper. We received countless hugs. As we pulled away, a sea of beautiful, brown, smiling faces abounding with laughter ran after our van.

We were all on such a high as we exited the camp. Our host then decided to stop at a random hut and asked permission for us to visit. He wanted us to "see" to have a better understanding of where and how many of these children lived, beyond our just peering at the landscape as we drove. The young mom who lived there seemed excited to have visitors. She asked for a moment. I thought she was going to tidy up, but later I realized she was moving a sick, sleeping child behind a small curtain at the rear of her small tent.

As I got out of the van, that child's twin, a toddler, ran up to me with her arms held high. I immediately scooped her up. She was wearing only a paper-thin dress—no diaper, no panties. Her hard-distended belly was a clear sign of starvation. She was so light, a vast difference from when I scoop up my grandson Clark whose weight tires my arms quickly. He was younger than this child I was holding, yet much bigger and heavier.

This was the home of a twenty-six-year-old refugee mom. She had four children and was also pregnant. Her entire home was not much bigger than my granddaughter's play pop-up tent. She was from the Congo. My conversations with locals echoed what I read in a *Newsweek* article from June 2017. In approximately one year, 1.3 million people had been displaced from the Congo, fleeing a very complicated civil war. This country was already one of the poorest in the world, ranking 176 out of 188 countries. Thousands were dying in the conflict. There was a lack of food, as well as many homes being destroyed. By May 2016, as many as 8,000 people a day had to leave their homes. Many crossed over into neighboring countries and settled in refugee camps, such as the one we were visiting, until it was safe to return.

This family was one of those thousands. However, it was no longer just a story I read or a situation I knew about. As I held and gently patted the back of this starving toddler, we spoke with her overwhelmed mother. Her husband had been gone for quite some time, longer than she had been pregnant. I later wondered: *Was she raped? Was she doing what she felt she needed to do to get food for her children?*

I will never know the answer to those questions.

This was an unplanned detour. My mind flooded with regret that I was not prepared. I had very little with me to offer this family. The team scoured the van to grab what we could: crackers, candy, baby wipes, a few small items, and a little money—but nothing that would really change her situation. I almost immediately began to make mental notes of preparing gift packages with practical items. But again, that would have made me feel better, but it would not have changed her situation.

This was a harsh reality. Only one of her children was old enough to go to school and join the 33,000 children enrolled in the feeding program. She did receive a ration of rice and water monthly from the camp authorities. Her rations were only enough for two weeks, though, and she had to make it stretch. Clearly, it was not working. Her children were starving.

When I think back to holding that starving baby, *I have to choose to trust God* in the situation. Please do not misunderstand me: I do not believe that evil actions are God's will. People have free choice. They can choose to act outside of God's laws, and their actions have a ripple effect. The evil that is taking place in the Congo—what forced that young mother to flee with her four small children, ultimately putting her in a situation where she was unable to provide for their needs— was not God's perfect plan for this little family. But I choose to *trust* in the Lord. I *trust* that He will give peace or provide provisions, or maybe that sweet little baby is already in the arms of Jesus and has started living her eternal life in heaven a little sooner than others. My mother's heart is never comfortable with the loss of life of a young child, but my spiritual heart has a little glimpse of how joyful it must be to dwell in Heaven.

I choose to trust in the Lord.

Trust in the Lord with all your heart, and do not lean on your own understanding. In all your ways acknowledge him, and he will make straight your paths. —Proverbs 3:5-6

Chapter 10

Do Good!

*Trust in the Lord, and do good; dwell in the land
and befriend faithfulness.* —Psalm 37:3

The next "do" on my list is "Do Good!" Now, this is
where the actions can go crazy. Scripture even tells us not to
grow weary in well doing (Galatians 6:9). However, when I
was seeking for answers and I read this verse, I felt like the
Lord was telling me to simplify it.

I do not think that I am to add an endless list of good
activities to my life. However, for me, I think it meant to
simply incorporate "doing good" as a part of *everyday life*. Stay
aware and open to opportunities to do good as the Lord
brings those opportunities our way.

It can be as simple as opening the door for someone,
sending an encouraging card, being patient with a slow
cashier, letting someone cut in front of you on a busy
highway, taking food to a local pantry, watching a neighbor's
child, noticing the forgotten, giving a smile, or taking a
moment to call and speak an encouraging word. Everyone,
young and old, can do this. It costs nothing, yet adds great
value.

I can deliver cookies to the local police officers on

Christmas Eve, or simply take a moment to thank an officer when I see one during my day. It doesn't have to be complicated. I taught my children a scripture verse when they were growing up: "Be kind to one another, tenderhearted, forgiving one another, as God in Christ forgave you" (Ephesians 4:32).

This simple thing that I could do helped me combat the paralysis that I was feeling. Even though the problems of this world are huge, the small acts of kindness and the choice to incorporate doing good into daily life will chip away at the monster.

The opportunities to do good that the Lord brings to me may look different than the opportunities He will present to you. We each have different talents and resources. When I need help with a sewing project, I call on my neighbor. She always comes to my rescue and easily fixes what I am unable to do. You would never call on me to help with sewing or to make any type of complicated food!

I recently took a call from a man who was looking for some supplies. He said he was going to a camp in Greece. I asked where, and it was Camp Moria, of course. When I told him I had been to that camp, there was an instant connection. He reported that the moms were given five cloth diapers a week for their infants. I knew firsthand of the water situation—or lack of water, really—to wash the diapers. Through my own social media accounts, I was able to collect some disposable diapers and cash to help with the man's bag fees. It was a small gesture, but I can send a few thousand diapers. It didn't solve the problem, but it did some good. The task was easy for me, but my sewing neighbor said it would have totally overwhelmed her.

My daughter, Alysse, is a teacher and has been deeply

affected by the rash of school shootings in the United States. She could have lived in a constant state of fretting, but she instead focused her energy on raising funds for a special doorstop that makes it easy for teachers to secure their rooms during a shooting. My son, AJ, was a police officer. After one of the fatal officer shootings, along with other efforts, my daughter-in-law, Megan, helped organize a gift card tree for the family of the fallen officer. I know that acts of doing good and acts of kindness are powerful. I personally think it is one of the most powerful, yet simple, tools we possess as believers.

I recently interacted with a man from Pakistan who is currently living in the Middle East. He met Christians there and said that their acts of kindness caused him to want to know more about their faith. He began to read "their" Bible. Soon after, he became a believer in Jesus and started taking discipleship classes. He was preparing to go on a mission trip to share that kindness with others, and he was excited to "do good."

The pastor I mentioned in the previous chapter with the feeding program in Uganda started with one school. Now, Pastor Solomon has an incredible feeding program. At this writing, the program is only five years old, but it feeds 33,000 children a day. That is not a misprint! It was up from 20,000 the previous year. Can you imagine feeding 33,000 children a day? I had been aware of Pastor Solomon's ministry and statistics for a few years and had helped mobilize teams to serve with his organization. I'd met with him when he came to the United States, and I was very excited to experience his ministry firsthand. I really wanted to understand *how* you feed 33,000 children a day.

When I visited in August 2016, the following were the

feeding program's basic details: They accomplish the daily feeding with a total staff of less than fifty people. The ministry serves in two refugee camps, Rwamwanja and Kiryandongo, both UNHCR-managed refugee settlement camps. Rwamwanja had more than 20,000 people, mainly from the Democratic Republic of Congo. It was nearly forty-two square miles then, and it kept growing, according to UNHCR reports. At that time, Kiryandongo had 60,000 people! They are refugees mainly from the South Sudan with others from Kenya, Democratic Republic of Congo, Rwanda, and Burundi.

Between the two camps, this organization serves at seventeen schools during their lunch times. Most schools have two cooks, although one has five cooks because of their large population. The program intentionally hires both a local Ugandan and a refugee living in the camp. The cooks always test the food before feeding it to the children.

Both camps have two people who oversee the overall process to make sure the food is not stolen and is distributed according to procedures. A total of three administrative staff help clear the food through the customs process. The supplies are minimal, and when I say *minimal*, I mean *minimal!* In addition to the food, they purchase wood for cooking, huge pots to cook in, and buckets from which to serve. That's it. There are no cups, plates, spoons, or forks provided, because food is the priority.

Their method is very different than the way my Western brain works. I would have thought of a list of "necessary" items, none of which is on their list. Possibly while waiting to assemble that "necessary" list of mine, fewer children would have been served and many children may have starved. It is a blessing to see the difference in the recipients as these workers nourish formerly starving children.

On the day I was serving with the program, I took my spot at the camp. We were stationed at various classroom doors. They brought us huge pots of the rice mixture and a big spoon. The beautiful faces of the children expressed such gratitude. The students said, "Thank you," one by one, as they were served their daily portion. For most children, this was their only meal. We served the very hot rice and dried vegetable mixture on whatever the students offered to us. A few had a cup or bowl, some had lids, but the majority put a piece of notebook paper on top of a school book. Those with no books asked their friends for a piece of paper. When one child cupped his hands for the rice, I couldn't bear to put the food into them, knowing how very hot it was and how it would burn his hands. I scanned the room and retrieved a dirty piece of paper from the floor, hesitated, then handed it to the young child and quickly served him his portion of the hot rice. He was just one of many to cup his or her hands in front of us that day.

This daily task is an incredible thing to do. Planning how to feed 33,000 children a day would completely overwhelm me, but Pastor Solomon was equipped to do it. Even so, there was something that our small team of eight visitors could do. That night, we purchased hundreds of plates. We determined to return to the school the following day with stacks of plates. Never had I seen a child shout with such glee when they received a plate—not a special plate with princesses or superhero characters—just a simple plate.

We entered the classrooms with plates in hand, and the children shouted with excitement. I fought back the tears as we passed plates to every child, such joy was given. The children waved their new plates in the air, shouting and laughing. This image is forever ingrained in my memories. The joy was indescribable. It was just a simple plate.

At another camp later that day, we fed thousands of children, and once again I was putting hot food on paper or cardboard. Many came with cupped hands. There was so much need, and we had no more funds for plates. But we did the good we could do, and I choose to trust God with the rest.

For I was hungry and you gave me food, I was thirsty
and you gave me drink, I was a stranger and you welcomed me.
—Matthew 25:35

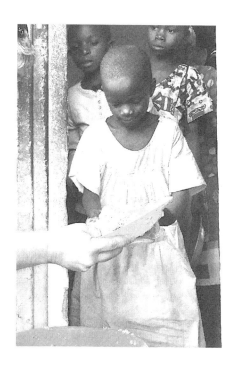

Chapter 11

Dwell in the Land!

Trust in the Lord, and do good;
dwell in the land and befriend faithfulness.
—Psalm 37:3

The fourth "do" on my list was to "Dwell in the land." These four simple words may not mean much to others, but they were very freeing to me in my previous state. They gave me permission to dwell in my land, to enjoy the blessings of the life that I have.

I can indulge and play with my grandbabies, eat out with my husband, and rest at the beach—all with no guilt, but simply with gratitude. When you travel to so many countries and see the poverty and hardships around the globe, it can be unsettling to come back to a life of abundance. One sometimes feels a sense of guilt. I have heard many mission team members ask, "How was I so lucky to be born in the United States?" We are blessed, but we do not have to feel guilty, just grateful. This is our land, and God gives us permission to dwell in it and to enjoy it.

I grew up in a modest home. I always had what I needed, and I had loving parents. Still, I was always aware that our standard of living was less than most people around me.

When we got married, Greg and I worked very hard. We were blessed in many ways and became financially secure. After a while, I no longer had to worry about having enough money to pay our bills. Eventually, we were able to buy a condo at the beach, a lifelong dream of mine. I relax best at the ocean. I am listening to the waves as I write this book. For a long time, though, I was almost embarrassed to tell people we had this little getaway. How can I spend time with the poor in Haiti or India or Honduras or anywhere, then come back to my life and not feel guilty?

These four words helped me to understand that I had permission to dwell in the land that the Lord gave me. I have never believed that possessions make one happy. If that were the case, then we're serving a cruel God. A great percentage of the world lives in poverty and that would sentence them to a life without happiness. It is simply not the case. I have seen great joy emanate from people with few possessions, and I have seen great sadness and frustration in those we consider wealthy.

Again, I had to make it simple. If I tithe, give offerings, and ensure that people are more important than things, then I can dwell in my land in peace and enjoy His blessing. I want to take this a step further: I believe in addition to enjoying the land we dwell in, we have a responsibility to pray for our land. I dwell in my physical house. I don't just enjoy it. I have to clean it. I make repairs. I invite people into it. My home helps me to function. I eat, sleep, and rest there. I have similar responsibilities to the country where I dwell.

For years, I've kept a prayer journal. Generally, I update it each January with various names to pray for. I always have a section for our government leaders: president, vice president, my state governor, mayor, senators, and congressional leaders. While I may or may not have voted for those individuals, the Bible commands me to pray for them. I try to educate myself on the issues, and I vote. I will not argue, and as part of dwelling in my land, I pray for our leaders.

Because my children are grown, I have some freedom in my schedule that I did not have when we were shuttling them from school events to sports and to church. I've audited a class on refugee issues at a local university; I have attended events designed to educate on local issues, such as affordable housing and upward mobility. When available, I try to attend forums on hard topics, such as race relations. It's all a part of how I dwell in my land. Others may staff polling locations, volunteer for a political candidate, or even participate in a peaceful protest. All are ways to dwell in your land. We do not need to feel guilty—just grateful, and enjoy dwelling in our land!

First of all, then, I urge that supplications, prayers, intercessions, and thanksgivings be made for all people, for kings and all who are in high positions, that we may lead a peaceful and quiet life, godly and dignified in every way. —1 Timothy 2:1-2

Taking grandkids to the beach

My newest granddaughter

Chapter 12

Befriend Faithfulness!

Trust in the Lord, and do good;
dwell in the land and befriend faithfulness.
—Psalm 37:3

The final "do" is to "remain faithful." It sounds easy but seems rare. I had the privilege of attending the calling hours for the Reverend Billy Graham. He and Corrie ten Boom have always been my modern-day, all-time heroes of the faith. Billy Graham's life inspired me—all of his crusades and the thousands and thousands that came to an understanding of the Gospel through his ministry. However, his faithfulness through the years seemed to speak the loudest. Even the most cynical journalists commented on his life well lived. His life was an incredible testimony to the world and to his family of a genuine relationship with Christ. The eulogies his children gave were a testament to his faithfulness. His main goal in life was to hear from his heavenly father the words of Matthew 25:21: "His master said to him, 'Well done, good and faithful servant. You have been faithful over a little; I will set you over much. Enter into the joy of your master.'" I truly believe that is exactly what he heard on February 21, 2018.

Recently, I was at a gathering with some friends. I caught

up with a sweet woman with whom I had attended church for many years. She's at least ten years older than I am. I was inquiring about others in her circle who used to attend church with us. I was so saddened as I learned of some of their current situations. My heart aches every time there is a story of a pastor participating in such things as adultery or embezzlement. They have not been able to befriend faithfulness. I know this can sound judgmental—and I do not claim to know another person's heart, neither will I claim to judge their salvation. That's not my role. I am very grateful for the redemptive power of God when we fail. However, I also know there is great power in the testimony of a faithful servant that can speak very loudly to others and most importantly to their family members. This is my deepest desire, for my grandchildren to see a testimony of the power of befriending faithfulness and the blessings of the Lord.

I've served with incredible people who have lived a life of faithfulness, people like Caroline, Mama Jesse, Ron and Grace, and Laura. All are in their seventies, and they all still travel on missions, using their skills and talents domestically and internationally.

The first time I visited Cuba, I was surprised at the size of the church campus. On the first note of the first song the entire congregation erupted in worship. The team of eight young women, all dressed in white, elegantly danced on the stage as a full worship band skillfully played their instruments. This was certainly a successful church in the middle of Cuba. Later, I was able to sit and visit with the husband and wife who pastor this church. They are now in their seventies. They suffered during the revolution. For almost fifty years, they pastored this church, and for seventeen of those years had less than fifteen people. Several of those were family members. I am sure they could have justified closing the doors of the church many times. After all, it was not growing! There was persecution, little to no resources, and they had connections to go to America. However, they knew the Lord was telling them to remain faithful to *this* church. It is amazing how vibrant the church is today. In addition to a main campus of hundreds of members, they have also planted forty house churches. This church now reaches thousands. They pay for the church staff at the main campus, as well as forty house pastors. Each pastor makes the same salary, regardless of church size. They operate a conference center for youth activities and a training center for pastors. As an outreach, they have installed a computer lab that offers training to the community. None of this would have happened if they had not remained faithful. I am sure during those seventeen years of a congregation of fifteen people, they never imagined it would grow to what it is today. And it would not have, if they had not befriended faithfulness.

My missionary friends in Kyrgyzstan are retired schoolteachers, but they have a second career. They have a delightful cottage on a lake in Canada. They go and dwell there when they can, but it seems only long enough to re-energize and travel halfway around the globe to educate people on proper orphan care. They work for months at a time, not weeks.

While I was with them in Kyrgyzstan, the wife's 85-year-old mother—also a grandmother and great-grandmother—arrived from Texas. I was half her age, and I was still recovering from the long journey. I know how taxing a trip like that can be. Still, she spent two weeks teaching orphans how to sew. She moved slowly at times and may have gone to bed earlier than the rest of the group, but she was making a difference. She passed away later that same year, but I saw her befriending faithfulness and serving the Lord with her last breath.

My life verse is: "So as to walk in a manner worthy of the Lord, fully pleasing to him: bearing fruit in every good work and increasing in the knowledge of God" (Colossians 1:10). Not everyone is called to international service; however, every believer is called to remain faithful to whatever the Lord has called them.

It can be a prayer ministry. As my friend Anna aged, she was no longer able to help with the many church activities that she had done so faithfully. When I was busy serving on church staff and responsible for multiple activities, she made yummy homemade food for my husband and me and had her daughter bring it to me. She did simple projects like request that I bring the plastic eggs to her to stuff for the hundreds of kids attending the Easter egg hunt each year. She called me consistently for my prayer requests, and I knew she was sincerely praying for me. She sent cards of encouragement. She was a true blessing to me during my seventeen years on staff at the church. She befriended faithfulness!

I have been fortunate to interact with many over the years who have befriended faithfulness. I appreciate those with the gift of hospitality—those who will hold babies in a church nursery, praying over them, and giving relief to their tired mommies Sunday after Sunday. One friend has been setting up a church service under a bridge in Charlotte, N.C., and feeding the homeless every Sunday for the last twenty-one years. Cecil Newman, a woman who attends my mother's church, is eighty-nine years old. Upon learning that I was going to take feminine hygiene kits on various trips, she personally sewed and donated a hundred bags! I am blessed to see my own mother now in her seventies and still active in her church. While she doesn't travel internationally, she helps with the missions committee, assists with Vacation Bible School, visits the shut-ins, and volunteers for other church activities. She is quick to bring a meal to someone in need or offer a ride to church to those who can't drive. These are faithful servants.

I have the same desire as Billy Graham to hear those words at the end of my life: "Well done, thou good and faithful servant." As much as I desire to hear those words for myself, I also pray fervently that my children and grandchildren will hear those words at the end of their lives, too. I may not always understand everything about this life, but I choose to remain faithful to my God. When I fail (and I will fail), I will ask for forgiveness and then keep going. I choose to befriend faithfulness.

But the fruit of the Spirit is love, joy, peace, patience, kindness, goodness, faithfulness, gentleness, self-control; against such things there is no law.
—Galatians 5:22-23

Church in Cuba

Chapter 13

A Return to Hope

For his anger is but for a moment and his favor is for a lifetime.
Weeping may tarry for the night, but joy comes with the morning.
—Psalm 30:5

I continue to follow up with my friends around the globe.
Pastor Solomon is still feeding thousands in Uganda. He is
planting churches and ministering on the airwaves. His
organization disciples thousands. Pastor Bob is in his
fourteenth year equipping and growing the church in
Morocco. His work is sensitive, and I can't say much, but
numbers are being added to the Kingdom daily.

At this writing, a school is nearly completed in the village
where I served in Botswana. The children in this village will
no longer be transported to a boarding school to receive their
education. This makes my heart sing! A ministry has started
regular meetings for the teen moms. They offer spiritual,
physical, and emotional support. There is also training
available that will enable leaders to meet the needs of
traumatized children. This is all happening deep in the bush
of Africa.

I also recently returned to Greece and served at a refugee
help center in Athens. The atmosphere was completely
different from my original experience. Hope was abundant.

In the midst of the feeding program, shoe distributions, language classes, and various discipleship classes, we were invited to a mid-week worship service. When my group arrived, the door was locked behind us. The room was packed with hundreds. They requested that we take no photos because former Muslims would be baptized, and they didn't want to risk something being posted to social media. The individuals wanted the opportunity to tell their families about their newfound faith on their own terms. I was, however, permitted to take a photo of the baptism tank. My heart leaps for joy every time I see that picture and remember those who were baptized. I literally felt like I was in a church in the book of Acts. When the new believers came up out of the water, tears were streaming down their faces. In my mind, their faces were glowing, almost shining.

I loved hearing their testimonies about coming on a boat and getting stuck in Greece. Some were even in Camp Moria when I was. Now, through the kindness of the believers they met along the way, they have found salvation. As awful as the conflict is that caused the displacement of entire people groups, God is working in this crisis to bring people to Him. These are people who may have never had the opportunity to hear the Gospel had their lives not been totally disrupted.

The group I was serving with not only had people from the USA but six believers from Hong Kong. A man from Switzerland and another from Germany also joined us. Those who ran the center were from Iran. Every day, we had morning devotions together. There were Bibles in multiple languages. Each person took a turn sharing, then praying in his or her native language. The last night, we rejoiced together. After sharing a traditional meal, we had a dance party. Yes, you read that right. It was a celebration of our time together. The music was very Middle Eastern, and it was fun. It was pure joy. I realized that I had been shortsighted in my first encounters. God was not done working; the story is still not complete. It never will be, until the day of His return.

I was a children's pastor for many years. I have tried to not make the Gospel complicated. Maybe that's why these three simple verses from Psalm 37 have helped so much in my journey. It was something practical, something easy, something I could do when there was so much I could do nothing about. I hope that they help you, too, as you process your journey.

I am highly aware that on my own, I would be tempted to veg out in front of the TV, watch hours of *Shark Tank* and HGTV, fritter away time on Facebook or Pinterest, go to the movies or out to eat with friends, and go shopping. There is nothing wrong with any of those things. However, it cannot be my entire life. That would be tapping out on the life God has for me—and for you! It is only with the grace of God and by His power that we are able to embrace the knowledge of the unfair and through Him strive to make a difference. May we, with the Lord's strength, be faithful.

It may not be easy. You may be taken advantage of, let down, disappointed, inconvenienced. It may cost you money or time. In fact, I guarantee it will require both. However, I wholeheartedly believe that if you live by Godly principles, not only will you get a glimpse of how wonderful and beautiful eternity will be, you will also enjoy a fulfilled and satisfied life, one that makes a difference in those around you. Your life will bring glory to the Lord. It will be an imperfect life, one with failure, but it will be a life that is not spent fretting because of evil. You will **trust** in the Lord, **do good**, **dwell** in the land, and be **faithful.**

I *will* continue my Journey. I hope *you* will continue your Journey as well!

May the God of hope fill you with all joy and peace in believing, so that by the power of the Holy Spirit you may abound in hope.
—Romans 15:13

Part Two

Encouraging Stories During

the Journeys:

I witness greatness as I serve with angels!

Story 1

Listen up!

My sheep hear my voice, and I know them, and they follow me.
—John 10:27

On my January 2015 trip to Honduras, I was privileged to have a team member named Carlos. Carlos grew up poor in El Salvador. His English was a bit broken, and he was going to be our interpreter for the team. He worked as a maintenance man at a local school in my community. It was laid on someone's heart to pay his way and invite him to travel with our group. At our team meeting, Carlos shared how he received his first pair of shoes at age eight and what that gift meant to him. He was now very excited to have the opportunity to give shoes to children who were now growing up as he did.

At our first shoe distribution I was sitting at one end of a row of seats, and Carlos at the other end, with about fifteen people between us. In an instant, the Holy Spirit spoke to my heart, "Stop! Go take a photo of Carlos." I quickly finished what I was doing. I sensed an urgency to get that photo now. I almost dismissed that thought, as it made more sense for me to remain seated and to continue to serve. But I listened to that voice, and I'm so glad that I did!

At that moment, Carlos was washing the feet of a small boy. I asked the boy how old he was, and he replied that he was eight years old. Then, Carlos asked him his name, and his name was *Carlos!* At the very moment the Holy Spirit told me to go take a photo of Carlos, he was serving an eight-year-old boy named Carlos! I said to the adult Carlos, "Tell him your story!" Who better to encourage this young boy, than someone who was just like him? As adult Carlos began to share, he became emotional and began to cry. Adult Carlos recognized the significance of that moment. Then, the child Carlos replied: "Don't cry. I'm happy. I'm getting my shoes today!"

Adult Carlos said, "I know you are happy," as he knew *exactly* how that young boy felt. He was able to continue to have a very meaningful conversation with young Carlos.

This experience only reinforces that we serve a big God. A God who cares about the individual. There were about 400 children at this event. The chances of me getting up and taking a photo at the very moment Carlos was with Carlos are nearly impossible. Add the fact that the young Carlos actually sat in front of adult Carlos when there were fifteen other seats—again, nearly impossible. This moment forever encouraged the adult Carlos, myself, and the rest of our team, as well as the child Carlos! I love that I serve a God that is always working out the impossible if we are aware enough to listen!

Unfortunately, I am sure that I have heard that voice in the past and dismissed it, rationalized it away, and missed a blessing or missed an opportunity to bless others. It should not be a rare occurrence to hear God's voice, follow His instructions, and see His incredible hand at work. The Bible is full of examples of people hearing the voice of God:

Noah

"And God said to Noah, 'I have determined to make an end of all flesh, for the earth is filled with violence through them. Behold, I will destroy them with the earth.'"
—Genesis 6:13

Moses

"When the Lord saw that he turned aside to see, God called to him out of the bush, 'Moses, Moses!' And he said, 'Here I am.'" —Exodus 3:4

The Widow of Zarephath

"I have commanded a widow there to provide for you."
– 1 Kings 17:9

Samuel

"The word of the Lord came to Samuel."
—1 Samuel 15:10

Mary

"Then the angel said to her, 'Do not be afraid Mary, for you have found favor with God.'" – Luke 1:30

Phillip

"Now an angel of the Lord said to Philip, 'Rise and go toward the south to the road that goes down from Jerusalem to Gaza.' This is a desert place." —Acts 8:26

Saul/Paul

"And falling to the ground, he heard a voice saying to him, 'Saul, Saul, why are you persecuting me?' And he said,

'Who are you, Lord?' And he said, 'I am Jesus, whom you are persecuting. But rise and enter the city, and you will be told what you are to do.'" —Acts 9:4-6

Ananias

"Now there was a disciple at Damascus named Ananias. The Lord said to him in a vision, 'Ananias.' And he said, 'Here I am, Lord.' And the Lord said to him, 'Rise and go to the street called Straight, and at the house of Judas look for a man of Tarsus named Saul, for behold, he is praying.'" —Acts 9:10-11

Just to name a few! I encourage you today to invite the Lord to speak to you. Then listen ... then obey ... and experience the presence of the Lord at work, here, now, today in your life.

Adult Carlos with child Carlos

Story 2

What Woman Doesn't Need a New Pair of Shoes?

For the needy shall not always be forgotten,
and the hope of the poor shall not perish forever.
—Psalm 9:18

In January 2014, I was planning a shoe distribution trip to India. When I received the itinerary, I noticed that we were going to visit a women's HIV Clinic. I had received the shoe sizes for most of the other distribution sites but not for this particular one. When I asked the Indian missionary about the shoes for the clinic he responded, "Women do not need shoes." I was shocked. I explained again that it is not just about receiving shoes, but it is our way of showing love, an act of servant leadership, and we wanted to serve the ladies. Once more I was told, "Women don't need shoes." Finally, on my third ask, I was told we could bring the ladies "slippers," which meant flip-flops.

I was a bit irritated: We were giving nice shoes to the pastors and the children, but only flip-flops to the women at the clinic. We did have a large donation of new flip-flops in the warehouse, so I was able to bring what they requested.

Once in India, the night prior to the distribution, I had an idea. I asked all the team members to bring any nail polish they had. We gathered several bottles. Knowing that we were going to distribute flip-flops, I thought we could make this more of a "spa experience" and offer a station for the women to get their nails painted if they liked.

When we arrived at the clinic the following day, it was nothing like I had imagined. I imagined a somber, sterile, doctor's office waiting area. Instead, it was the back yard of a church. The women were already gathered, sitting on the ground. The area was separated by colorful tarps. The women were singing, and I soon saw that this was a very happy place. Most of these women were considered "untouchables."

Though the constitution of India has officially abolished "untouchability," the reality is that in many rural areas there is still such discrimination. This group is part of the Dalit community. In 2016, according to a report given by National Public Radio, there were still over 200 million people who were considered untouchables. They often perform jobs considered some of the dirtiest occupations, such as street sweepers and waste removal. The women shared with us how even in their own communities, they were not given a cup of water on a hot day.

The definition of the word *Dalit* comes from a Hindu word meaning "oppressed, suppressed, downtrodden." However, at this "clinic," one day a week, these women did not look "oppressed, suppressed, or downtrodden!" The women met to sing, see their friends, share a meal, study the Bible, and pray. This was their happy day, and this certainly was a happy place. The medicines were in a small office, but all other activities were in this open-air courtyard. They received medicine, vitamins, rice, and oil. More important, they got to connect with friends and encourage one another in their walk with the Lord.

I stood in front of about a hundred ladies and began to explain what we were going to do: We would serve them, wash their feet, paint their toenails, and offer prayer. Immediately, they shook their heads no, explaining that they were not worthy and that they should wash our feet. I began again, this time making my talk more about *me*. "I will be so sad if we can't do this for you. We traveled a long way …" My interpreter then went on and on and on. I doubt that he was saying what I said, but, finally, the women consented.

The water was in a well too far and too precious for washing feet, so we used baby wipes. We also had hotel lotions, and we offered another station for their toes to be painted. *All* of the women chose to have their toes painted. It was so much fun. When the system was up and running, I sat down to serve a couple of women. The first two I served completely caught me off guard when they bowed down and *kissed* my feet! I gave them flip-flops. They *kissed* my feet!

This event was so *not* about the shoes. This was a time to remind the women that they are valuable and that God loves them. Their lives still mattered as untouchables, HIV-positive women in the middle of India.

As we were leaving, I asked the pastor in charge of the clinic about its success. He replied, "Since we began, about one year ago, we have seen seven ladies die. However, they all died with a smile on their face and the knowledge of Jesus as their Savior. It has been a great success!" And, oh, how I agree!

We all have periods of feeling unworthy, unusable, unloved. It is a lie. It is the opposite of what scripture teaches us. It paralyzes us and keeps us from enjoying all that God has for us. We may not need something as tangible as a stranger to come and wash our feet to remind us of our value; however, we all need reminding.

Scriptures to encourage your soul

And I am sure of this, that he who began a good work in you will bring it to completion at the day of Jesus Christ. —Philippians 1:6

Now, in all these things we are more than conquerors through him who loved us. —Romans 8:37

When you pass through the waters, I will be with you; and through the rivers, they shall not overwhelm you when you walk through fire you shall not be burned, and the flame shall not consume you. —Isaiah 43:2

So you will find favor and good success in the sight of God and man. —Proverbs 3:4

For you bless the righteous, O Lord; you cover him with favor as with a shield. —Psalm 5:12

… Teaching them to observe all that I have commanded you. And behold, I am with you always, to the end of the age. —Matthew 28:20

But they who wait for the Lord shall renew their strength; they shall mount up with wings like eagles they shall run and not be weary; they shall walk and not faint. — Isaiah 40:31

My daughter-in-law painted toenails

Story 3

The Miracle of the ~~Shoes~~

And taking the five loaves and the two fish, he looked up to heaven and said a blessing over them. Then he broke the loaves and gave them to the disciples to set before the crowd. And they all ate and were satisfied. And what was left over was picked up, twelve baskets of broken pieces.
—Luke 9:16-17

Kenya

When I was making our plans to serve in Kenya, the missionary asked if the team would be willing to camp. Actually, I am not a camper, but I asked the team, and the eight women were very excited.

We were going to camp for a couple of days, because the village that the missionary wanted us to serve was located too far from Nairobi to make the trip back and forth and have time to serve the students. We would work there for three days and camp for 2 nights.

The guides he hired to travel with us were wonderful. They set up our tents, cooked for us, and kept a fire going 24/7 to keep any wild animals away. The missionary was involved with a feeding program at this school, as well. Therefore, we would also help to measure and record the height and weight of each child. This information documented the difference the nutritious food was making.

When I saw the kids line up my heart sank. A much larger portion of the students looked older than I anticipated. Prior to our arrival I asked about the students' ages and was told this was an elementary and junior high school. But many of the students looked to be well into high school ages. I began to question that, and the explanation was: "If you start school, and you are eight years old, you are in grade one. If you start school and you are five years old, you are in grade one. If you have to stay home for a year and help your family, when you return, you begin in the grade you left." The classes are assembled by how many years one has been in school—not by age. By the eighth grade children could range from age thirteen to eighteen, and they did.

My concern grew. I hadn't brought enough larger size shoes. I felt that Day One and Day Two we would probably be fine. However, by Day Three, we were going to run out of needed sizes. This group was in *great* need. Many had no shoes, others were wearing mismatched shoes, and even more had the ends cut off of their shoes to allow for their growing feet. I had never seen so much need in one location.

On the last day, I told the team not to look at the sizes. We would simply ask our shoe-stock person to give us the largest size that they could find. We began joking, "Give me a magic nine," and "I need a magic ten," and so on. There was no village where I could go to purchase shoes. When we were out, we were done.

How heartbreaking it would be for this final very needy group—who were patient and who waited their turn to be served on the last day—to not receive shoes.

What happened next was a miracle.

At the end of this last day *every child* received a pair of shoes. It was truly like the story of Jesus and the loaves and fishes. Every time we needed a shoe, we found one in the shoe area. I looked at my team, and we were all in tears. We knew our inventory.

I began to interview a school administrator who had served with us all week. I have his interview on a video in my iPad. He began his statement saying: "Today, today I saw a miracle!" I was thinking, "That's right! We saw a miracle. We saw all these students receive shoes." Then he finished his sentence: "Today, I saw people washing feet. No matter how dirty the feet were, [the people] used their tender hands and prayed for us and washed our feet. Even our parents have not done this for us. We will remember forever this group coming and washing our feet and praying for us."

I train people all the time that this mission is not about the shoes. The shoes are a tool to have a conversation, to share words of encouragement. Again, I was in tears.

We had a hundred very small pairs of shoes left. The teacher told us of a little preschool right down the hillside. We arranged to go there and serve those little ones as well.

I promised the Lord I would share this miracle story.
The miracle of the shoes …
… no, actually, the miracle of a kind touch.

Belize

Blessed are the feet of those that bring good news! But, sometimes, those feet are bruised, sore, and infected. When a pastor in the jungles of Belize sat down in front of me, he warned me: "I have some problems with my feet." And he did. (No photos, just use your imagination.) I am very fortunate that this type of thing never bothers me. I simply proceed.

The ground there was so wet. Many of the roads were flooded. There is not really summer and winter. Instead, it is rainy or dry season. This was definitely the rainy season. The pastor had to walk from his home to the church across a flooded bridge. His tennis shoes were often soaked. This contributed to his foot issues. I knew I needed to give him the Samaritan's Feet World Shoes. These shoes look similar to a Croc-style shoe. However, they have an anti-microbial element that helps to protect feet against infections. This was one of our last distributions. I was told multiple times that we had *no* XL shoes left, before even arriving at this location. I knew just by looking at his feet, they would never fit into our only remaining large size. I simply prayed "God please help me find an 'extra-large.'" I felt compelled to get up and look. I walked over to a bag as if I had full confidence that the shoes I needed were in that bag. I dumped it out, and on the very bottom was one pair of XL! Superman with his X-ray vision couldn't have found those shoes. The pastor was so happy. I fitted him with the badly needed shoes. I prayed for him. My faith was built and so was his. God is so good.

Remember the wondrous works that he has done,
his miracles, and the judgments he uttered,
—Psalm 105:5

Camping in Kenya

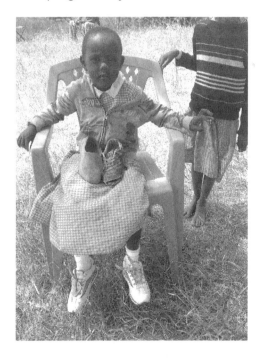

Pastor in Belize

Story 4

Sizes 8, 9, and 10

The heart of man plans his way, but the Lord establishes his steps.
—Proverbs 16:9

This was my second visit to Morocco. After my first visit,
I felt more prepared. I truly trained this team for a mission of
kindness. When dealing with refugees, one never knows how
many people we will actually serve. I packed tarps to create
imaginary rooms to help make the distributions orderly. I also
packed many more men's shoes.

We shipped bags of shoes to those whose travel did not
originate in Charlotte. My team members were coming from
various locations. One in particular was traveling from
Indiana. We had prepared, mainly through conference calls,
and the entire group met together for the first time in person
in New York. When the tickets were booked, I somehow
missed that during our layover in Paris, my Indiana team
member would not be on the same flight with the rest of the
team, but a later flight arriving about two hours after our
arrival.

When I noticed the oversight a couple days before
departure, I did everything I could think of to switch him to
our flight, but without success. I continued trying during our
trip, believing that a seat would open up on our plane. Yet,

much to my disappointment, we were not able to change his schedule. It was disappointing.

When the team arrived, the customs officials flagged our large bags. They were not persuaded by my usual paper work and insisted that I return on Monday. We arrived on Saturday. I explained that we had a shoe distribution planned for the following day, Sunday, and we really needed the shoes. They would not budge.

In the meantime, my solo teammate landed. He proceeded with no issues. His two large bags of shoes made it all the way through customs with him. That night, once we were settled and had our first team meeting, we decided to proceed to the small church on Sunday to attempt to do the shoe distribution as planned, with only the shoes from those two bags. I had actually packed those very bags weeks prior. I vividly remembered randomly choosing the shoes and saying a quick prayer before shipping them to Indiana.

Those bags contained only men's shoes, sizes 8, 9, and 10. That night, we prayed for all men with shoe sizes 8, 9, and 10. I believed but asked God to help my unbelief! My faith was so strong, that I immediately began to make alternative plans. (Sorry, Lord!) I explained to the team how we would take names of those we didn't have proper sizes for and when we had access to our detained shoes, we would pull those sizes and set them aside. We would work with the missionary to make arrangements to eventually deliver the shoes. Oh, ye of little faith!

We arrived for the Sunday evening service, and the congregation was almost entirely male! The two females in attendance were visiting from the US and were not in need of shoes—they only wanted prayer. As we began to serve the congregation, made up mainly of immigrants—you guessed it—every person was either a size 8, 9, or 10. We provided every single person with shoes that fit. What a miracle!

I look back and praise God that my team member's flight was not changed. I marvel that as I was in the warehouse in Charlotte gathering shoes in a random fashion, that I was unknowingly grabbing the exact sizes we would need for the first distribution. I was amazed that when we entered that small church, we had exactly what we needed in our small inventory of about fifty shoes.

I do not understand why this need was met so miraculously, while I have had other experiences when I was not able to meet the need. I am grateful for the experience as I marvel at the sovereignty of God.

While God also bore witness by signs and wonders and various miracles and by gifts of the Holy Spirit distributed according to his will.
—Hebrews 2:4

Story 5

Keep Dreaming!

May the God of hope fill you with all joy and peace in believing,
so that by the power of the Holy Spirit you may abound in hope.
—Romans 15:13

Haiti Mom

I had a conversation with a young woman who was around twenty years old. She didn't know her birthday. She had four children and was expecting child number five. I will repeat: She was only twenty. She slept with eight people in a dirt floor shack, with little protection from the rain. There was one bed. Most people in the shack slept on the floor. She was only able to stay in school until around age twelve. When asked what her hopes and dreams were, she had no reply for quite awhile, then said she could not think of any.

My heart ached for her. She was so young to have lost her ability to dream for a better life. But her hope and her dreams would soon be restored. She had no idea this village was going to be transformed over the next several months. God willing, resources would be raised for water, food, shelter, and more.

Even when one has lost dreams and feels forgotten, hope can be restored and dreams will come again. A couple years later a friend of mine was returning to this woman's village. I asked the friend to follow up. Her life had dramatically changed. She now had dreams for her children, dreams for a better life. I love that I serve a God who still has a future and a plan for us, even when we may not be able to see or understand that beautiful plan in our most desperate times.

Haiti Boy

Our team in Haiti served in a prison. It was a dark, depressing place. Often, one is put in prison and waits months until his or her trial. If you do not have any funds to pay fines, then you are also detained. Young boys and hardened criminals are housed in the same area of the prison.

One young man we served was thirteen years old. His crime was throwing rocks with other boys. A rock broke a windshield. The other boys ran, but he didn't run fast enough and was caught. His father knew he was in prison but did not have the needed money for the fine and damages—more than $300 U.S. The young man looked so scared. I would be scared, too. However, we were able to arrange payment and secure his release. What a difference two days made. He had no idea that strangers would come, serve him, hear his story, and arrange for his release. Like the young woman in the story above, he had lost hope. His own father was unable to help him. When he also lost his ability to dream, God had a plan and hope was restored to his life as well.

I am so grateful that I serve a living God that restores our hopes and dreams!

For the needy shall not always be forgotten,
and the hope of the poor shall not perish forever.
—Psalm 9:18

Story 6

Special Dinner Invitations

And the master said to the servant, 'Go out to the highways and hedges and compel people to come in, that my house may be filled.'
—Luke 14:23-24

Morocco

I have enjoyed many special dinner invitations around the globe. I've had high tea in London. I savored wonderful meals and the best macarons ever in Paris. I even drank real gold flakes in a cappuccino in Abu Dhabi. But the meals that really stand out to me are the many invitations from those with few resources, who gladly spend up to a week's wages to offer a meal and honor my teams and me. We experienced this in the Philippines, Brazil, and Cuba, among others. I know that this is a part of their way to honor our Lord by honoring our team.

One such memorable meal took place in the small apartment of a Muslim family in Casablanca. They were not Christians, but they spent several hours preparing a beautiful *tagine* dish. In addition, they arranged for an artist to come and offer intricate henna tattoos for the women.

The mother of this family worked as a cook for the missionary with whom we were serving. She heard what we were doing around the country and invited us to her home.

We had to say yes. The hospitality and conversation were fantastic. It took several hours.

In a situation like this, I would have an envelope with a substantial offering, wanting to cover the expense of the meal. I would find a way, often including it in a card given to the host. It was never expected, but I knew the sacrifice, and it made *me* and my team feel better. Hmm.

I quietly went into the kitchen and was about to give the offering, when a local friend who knew the customs intercepted me. "Teresa, if you offer that money to her, you will offend her. You must not do this!"

I quickly put the bills in my pocket and made some small talk in the kitchen. Offending our host was the last thing I wanted to do. It is so hard to receive from people who have much less than we do. But I also understand that serving us made them happy. It was a blessing to them to give. I didn't want to ruin that blessing. I just had to be uncomfortable. We would express our thankfulness in another way.

After dinner, we explained that we, too, had a gift. We wanted to wash their feet and fit them with new shoes. Soon, neighbors began to arrive. Amazingly, we had shoes for everyone—about seventeen in all. A replica of an open Quran was attached to the wall. The chair we used to pray, wash feet, and fit the new shoes was located directly under this art piece. We asked if we could pray, and again all were receptive. They knew we were Christians. We prayed in the name of Jesus. Some of them cried as they shared their prayer requests and then as we gently washed their feet. It was beautiful.

Their hospitality continued. When I thought I could eat no more, another tray of beautiful desserts and tea rounded out the experience.

This challenged me. I understand the financial sacrifice from my fellow believers. It is a way of supporting ministry and often a way of thanking those who come to serve their congregations. However, I think in most cases, if the church in the US asked us to host an entire team, many people would ask for a budget or reimbursement. We would never expect anyone here in the US (one of the richest nations in the world) to sacrifice an entire week's income to feed a group of strangers.

Now, let's take it a step further: What if we were asked to show such hospitality to people we disagree with theologically? Some of us have problems hosting a meal when the people we love have different political views. That night, we received an incredible act of kindness. I will learn from their example, and I will always pray for my Muslim friends.

Uganda

I don't know where to start with this story. The team was invited to the home of a pastor in Jinja, Uganda. I have a colleague who has done a lot of work in Uganda, and Pastor Simon was one of her friends. She had arranged this special invitation for my group. After we finished serving the children in a foster home, we began to make our way to his home. I knew it would be humble and small, but I was not prepared for what I experienced. The bus stopped at the bottom of a small hill overlooking the Nile River. The homes were similar to what I had seen in the slums of Nairobi. I now knew why we had to get off our bus. There was no possible road for such a vehicle in this community. We exited and began to follow the pastor as he weaved on small paths around the various homes. My mind was racing: *This can't be right.* The conditions were extremely harsh.

We stopped in front of a small wooden shack. We entered the darkened room. I'm ashamed to say my initial thoughts immediately went to the sanitation conditions and if the food would be safe to eat. After all, I was responsible for the well-being of this team. We didn't need exposure to typhoid or parasites. There was no kitchen inside. The women were cooking outside over a small fire. I later learned they had been cooking for hours. I also saw the source of their water, a small spigot located between the two huts.

The nine of us entered and were joined by a few others. The entire home would easily fit into my living room at home. I believe six children were living there with him and his wife; most were orphans, and one child had HIV and was recovering from malaria. They showed up at his door, and he took them into his two-room home.

The pastor began to share his calling to *this* community. He and his wife had *chosen* to relocate to this area. Initially, he traveled to and from the community, but then felt the conviction to live among the people to be able to impact this community.

"They needed a pastor," he said.

He planted a church in his home. The first week, he had five people. The second week, thirty people showed up. I can't believe thirty people could fit in his home. By the third week, they had to meet at the local school. The congregation is now over a hundred people per week. At this writing, it has probably grown well beyond those numbers. They have an average of five salvations a week. The pastor also became involved in the community's education system, and now he oversees a school of more than two hundred students. Our host on this trip was Pastor Solomon, a fellow Ugandan pastor. He too was touched, and said this was a great sacrifice by Ugandan standards, too.

Soon, dish after beautiful dish was set in front of us: meats, fruits, various rices, spinach, and more. This was the equivalent of two weeks' wages. How could we not eat? We blessed the food, and broke all the rules about what to eat and not eat in a foreign country. (Rule of thumb: If you don't cook it, boil it, or peel it yourself, don't eat it.) It was delicious. No one got sick.

Our group did not have much time; we had to leave right after dinner. We left a generous offering and a promise to minister together in the future. I am currently planning to send a team to serve with him for an entire week. We were also able to send additional funds from the US to help support a few special projects.

We were all humbled and touched by their commitment to this community. We discussed our inability to commit to living in such dire circumstances—even if we thought we might be able to manage—we would have difficulty asking this of our children, too. However, it was his *love* for these people that compelled him for the sake of the salvation of this community

This is a little like Jesus leaving heaven to come here for us. How could His heavenly Father ask him to do so? Yet, his *love* for our lost community compelled him, so we could have salvation. It is a rare privilege to meet someone who is so Christ-like—literally. I believe I have served at times with angels.

> *Do not neglect to show hospitality to strangers,*
> *for thereby some have entertained angels unawares.*
> —Hebrews 13:2

Dinner in Morocco

Simon's home, dinner in Uganda

Acknowledgements

I am grateful for my mom. (My friend!) I have seen her on her knees for me from the time I was a teenager, and she has continued to pray for me now that I'm a grandmother! I love you.

I want to thank Manny and Tracie Ohonme, founders of Samaritan's Feet. Your sacrifices and efforts are making an impact all over the globe. It has been a privilege to serve with you and to call you both my friends.

I want to thank my "Girl Friends!" You are my Prayer Partners and my Bible Study buddies, and, wow, have we done a lot of life together. I cherish our friendships: Kim, Pattie, Debbie, Rhonda, Jo Ellen, Cindy, Michelle, Carol, Tracey, and Karrie.

My Samaritan's Feet Family: Candy, Katherine, Davida, Shannon, Robyn, Deni, Denise, Whitney, Bryan, Larry and the rest of the beautiful team. I love you all.

I want to thank Kristen and Tim for their hard work in helping me to complete this project.

Thank you Pastor Everett … or should I say "Little Brother!" I am so glad that we have not just journeyed through childhood together, but we have had adventures as adults together. We never would have dreamed as small children that we would both serve all over the globe.

Chris, you're a more than a sister-in-law. You are a sister. I love you and am grateful for you.

My friends around the globe: Thank you for your

unending service. You have each contributed to my journey. I am so privileged to have met and served with each of you: Chris, Darrell, Justen and Sharon, Ruby, Solomon, Simon, Gina, Aphrodite, JP, Parissa, Mitra, and so many more.

My many teammates that have shared a journey or two with me: Many of you are now precious friends. I value our shared memories and remember so much laughter along the way.

My churches: Forest Hill Church and Barefoot Church. Thank you for praying for me each time I went on another journey.

Greg, you are the best husband, a cherished father, a phenomenal OD, and my best friend!

To my children: AJ, my superhero, strong and tender son, and Alysse, my passionate and caring daughter. You both have been my greatest joy. I am immeasurably proud of you. My best friends! (I'm allowed more than one best friend!)

Megan and Harry, you make our family complete. I always wanted four children, and now I have them. I love you both.

Lily, Isabel, Clark, and Violet, *this book is for you* to see God's faithfulness. I pray for each of you every day, and I always will. I look forward to celebrating each of your journeys with the Lord. In the end, your relationship with *Him* is all that will really matter. My love for each of you is massive and unconditional … and our heavenly Father loves you even more!

Be Significant!

My name is Teresa Hucko. I am a wife, Mother and Grammy. I grew up in a small town. I am probably the first in my family and extended family to have a passport. I've lived a very ordinary life: car pool, sports and practices with the kids, church activities. I juggled a job and home and found myself in the drive-through line at Chick-Fil-A more times than I care to admit.

However, I have had the privilege to travel to many parts of the world, mainly through my position with a faith-based non-profit organization, Samaritan's Feet. Many of the chapters in this book came from my experiences on my travels.

In the United States, we have, in my opinion, the false idea that fame equals significance. However, people become famous for many different reasons. With the invention of reality television, one can become famous for simply getting pregnant as a teen, purchasing a wedding dress, or for crazy antics along the Jersey shore.

I've served with, eaten with, and had meaningful conversations with people all around the globe doing truly significant work that no one knows about.

Pastor Solomon feeds 33,000 children a day—with no plates, cups, or spoons!

Ruby and Lynn refuse to retire, instead training thousands to be foster parents in the former Soviet Union. They are fighting for children in orphanages and institutions to have a family setting.

Pastor "Bob" rides a Harley though Morocco, providing relief to refugees, immigrants, and the underground church.

A church in India turns their backyard into an HIV clinic

for women with AIDS, and the untouchables receive love.

An 89-year-old great-grandmother traveled from Texas to Kyrgyzstan to teach girls how to sew so they will have a sustainable skill.

This list of those serving around the globe goes on and on. They are not famous, nor do they desire to be. They are simply significant!

Teresa Hucko
www.TeresaHucko.com

Made in the USA
Lexington, KY
13 November 2019